HOW TO GROW YOUR SMALL BUSINESS *RAPIDLY* ON-LINE

HOW TO GROW YOUR SMALL BUSINESS *RAPIDLY* ON-LINE

Cost-effective ways of making the internet really work for your business

JIM GREEN

howtobooks

Published by How To Books Ltd,
Spring Hill House, Spring Hill Road
Begbroke, Oxford OX5 1RX
Tel: (01865) 375794 Fax: (01865) 379162
email: info@howtobooks.co.uk
http://www.howtobooks.co.uk

First edition 2007

British Library Cataloguing in Publication Data
A catalogue record for this book is available from
the British Library.

ISBN 13: 978 1 84528 159 5

Produced for How To Books by Deer Park Productions, Tavistock
Typeset by *specialist* publishing services ltd, Montgomery
Cover design by Baseline Arts Ltd, Oxford
Printed and bound by Bell & Bain Ltd, Glasgow

Contents

Preface

If you run a small business of any description you may already have given some thought to online marketing. You might even have read up on the subject and been put off by what you gleaned. That is not surprising. Much of what is written about the internet marketplace is directed at big business and is, therefore, quite inappropriate for your circumstances. What is even more alarming is that some of it is just plain wrong.

The truth of the matter is that the internet is a mixture of brashness and subtlety that works only for those who understand the formula.

But when you learn how to recognise the disparate characteristics in action and know how to fuse them constructively from the point of view of the small business owner, you have at your command the most powerful and cost effective marketing device of the 21st Century.

The tragedy is, though, that many small businesses are still using the internet as a means of being seen to be 'doing something' online and so fail to take full advantage of the formidable and inexpensive range of electronic marketing tools and techniques available; resources that can mean the difference between maintaining a viable business or closing up shop; the difference that becomes singularly apparent when you become aware of its potency and apply its muscle to your own enterprise.

This pragmatic manual introduces you to a series of tried and tested strategies designed exclusively for modern small businesses and embryonic start-ups; strategies that work whether you simply wish to augment existing local sales potential or to be more adventurous and expand your enterprise into a global concern. Full of practical ideas on reaching new customers and increasing sales, this book will make a real difference in the success rate of small businesses and start-ups everywhere with little investment and even less risk.

Read on and prepare to be amazed at the array of income generating strategies and resources at your disposal – and all at a few flicks of the mouse button.

1
Using the internet for the purpose for which it was devised

Small business owners in the not-so-high streets of the 21st Century are facing greater challenges than ever before but ...

CAN YOU IMAGINE A WORSE CASE SCENARIO THAN THIS?

1. You own and operate a corner shop in Oswaldtwistle;

2. You know your customers by name by and large, and they know you;

3. Your stockholding is limited by reasons of available finance and storage space;

4. Your catchment area is shrinking by the minute;

5. You are surrounded by supermarkets with vast resources, bulk buying power and deep-cut pricing strategies;

6. You are under threat to your existence with the opening of *Oswaldtwistle Mills* at Junction7 off the M65 with its 80,000 square feet of retail shopping, free parking, coffee shops, restaurants, sweet factory, etc;

7. Your storefront is badly in need of refurbishment but you can't afford the expense of having it brought up to scratch;

8. You have to work all hours to maintain basic survival;

9. You've thought about selling out, but no one would buy;

10. You are approaching the end of your tether.

WHAT POSSIBLE USE IS THE INTERNET IN THESE CIRCUMSTANCES?

- How could it increase your customer base?

- How could it contribute to your till receipts?

- How could you learn how to use it?

- How could you use it when you don't even own a computer?

- How could it help you get more sales from your existing clientele?

- How could it help you get new customers?

- How could it help you compete with the multiples?

- How could it help you sustain your aspirations?

- How could it help you build the business so that one day you might be in a position to sell out?

- How could you afford to use it?

We'll talk more about the extreme scenario of the beleaguered Oswaldtwistle storekeeper in the next chapter, but meanwhile let's start by exploring the internet for the purpose it was devised. And as you read through the chapters to follow, you may be surprised at just how much that original purpose can do for you and your own small local enterprise.

USE THE WEB FOR THE PURPOSE FOR WHICH IT WAS DEVISED

Several decades ago the internet was first used by the Government of the United States of America with one dual purpose in mind:

- The electronic delivery of sensitive information;

- The receipt of equally sensitive data.

That purpose has not changed; it is the foundation stone on which all effective, dynamic online marketing is based. Nowadays, though, the impression is often that the internet has developed into an automatic electronic money-making machine. Not so, not now, not ever. Without question it is the most powerful and cost effective marketing device of the 21st Century, but you can only make it work when you know *why* it works.

MAKING THE INTERNET WORK FOR YOUR SMALL BUSINESS

- How do you do that?

- How do you make the internet work for you in your small business operation?

- And what's in it for you?

Here's how someone viewed the situation a few years back ...

> *If you're not doing business on the internet by the year 2000, you won't be doing business.*

> Bill Gates

Bill Gates' prediction failed to materialise. Perhaps he allowed personal vanity to overrule sanity because there are hundreds of thousands of commercial concerns worldwide who don't do any business online and yet continue to prosper.

But that does not mean to say that these businesses don't make best use of online marketing. Most of them do.

SO, HOW DO YOU MAKE ONLINE MARKETING WORK FOR YOU?

Use the internet for the purpose for which it was invented; use it as a channel of information.

- A channel for *receivable* information;
- A channel for *deliverable* information.

DOING IT THIS WAY PROVIDES YOU WITH TWO VALUABLE OPERATIONAL DEVICES

The facility to *receive* information opens the door to ongoing market research for even the smallest of enterprises, while the facility to *deliver* information electronically presents you with an internet marketing application with dynamic potential.

Using online search facilities …

- You can keep an eye on the marketplace, trends, and what the competition is up to;
- You can source valuable applications and software – and often for free;
- You can be on the lookout for trading opportunities.

Using the internet as a marketing application you can create a powerful website to:

- promote your small enterprise;
- promote your location;
- promote your merchandise;
- foster customer loyalty;
- service customer requirements;
- capture email addresses which build up into lists of potential customers.

You can do all of this – and if you go about matters in the right way, you can do it all for next to nothing in the way of investment – even if right now you don't know the difference between a keyboard and a washboard.

THE VALUE OF A GOOD WEBSITE TO THE SMALL BUSINESS OWNER

These are the benefits you should be looking to gain from your small business website: a fusion of incoming and outgoing information, intelligence that you should embrace to service existing customers and attract new ones. And unlike printed matter, you need never be nervous about imparting sensitive information (price lists, specifications, etc.) because you have the possibility to update variable data instantly.

As for direct selling, you'll get the odd sale or two from your site, but not a lot. Not yet anyway. Stick with it, though, and you'll do much more direct selling in time as the retail ethos of the web begins to bite – and there is evidence that it is starting to do just that – for even the smallest of trading concerns.

An *Ernst & Young* Study showed that in the year 2000 online retail sales were just above the $39 billion mark and have continued to rise year on year. Online retail sales in 2004 rose 23.8% to $89 billion, representing 4.6% of total global retail sales. Online retail sales were forecast to reach $109.6 billion by the end of 2005. (*Source Shop.org/Forrester*)

HOW IT ALL PANS OUT IN THE CREATION OF THE SITE

- Your mission statement and complementary graphics on the home page – where you would also position an 'order' button if required;

- Appropriate content for the pages devoted to produce, sales and service;

- Something of value for your website visitors – useful tips on your particular area of expertise: suggestions which should be updated on a regular basis;

- Links from one page to another within your site – but not beyond – or you'll lose your precious visitors to someone else;

- An electronic 'forum' where visitors can clock in and record comments;

- An email address where they can contact you;

- A facility to which you should give serious consideration straightaway: an invitation to subscribe to your free newsletter.

Okay, there's some work involved in setting up your virtual stall and in particular servicing the final item listed – but it will be worth it – because electronic newsletters ('ezines') are the best way to capture email addresses, build up a prospects list, and create new customers.

As to costs for website creation and hosting: very little, if you use a service such as Third Sphere which is devoted to fostering small business online.

http://thirdspherehosting.com/plus/?xstcreat&id=xstcreat&pkg=

WHAT YOU GET WITH THE THIRD SPHERE LOCAL ENTERPRISE HOSTING SERVICE

1. Choice of fonts;

2. Point-and-click web page creation software;

3. Context-sensitive menus when building;

4. Common Gateway Interface (CGI) bin;

5. CGI scripts library;

6. Graphics library;

7. Uploading to server;

8. Password protected pages;

9. Custom error pages;

10. Backup system;

11. Source code editing;

12. Spell check;

13. Spam blockers;

14. Total marketing automation;

15. Traffic centre + tools;

16. Upload files *without* File Transfer Protocol (FTP);

17. Edit HTML on screen;

18. Anti-virus software;

19. Secure space (product delivery);

20. PDF ebook creator (ex WORD files).

If you spend $25 (approx. £15) a month with them, they'll give you advanced tools to create a website which looks as though it cost £25,000 to construct.

KEEPING PACE WITH THE INTERNET OPPORTUNITY

Despite the bad publicity associated with the collapse of numerous major dot.coms in recent times, the internet is still in its infancy, but even so offers an incredible opportunity to small business – if small business would take the trouble to discover how best to use the internet to its *current* advantage. In so doing, small businesses will be operating on a universal platform and on equal status to the major players. That said, unless yours is a downloadable product or service, you won't be doing much in the way of direct selling (not yet anyway) but you will move with the times and *carve out a niche for yourself* in other essential directions.

LOCAL OFFLINE BUSINESSES GROW RAPIDLY ONLINE

If you own an offline business with local clientele, a website is a must nowadays. Use it to grow your business locally, build trust and deepen relationships with existing local customers, raise your local profile above that of competitors, keep your customers in touch through your ezine, attract new customers, and in many cases extend your market globally. Your world, your reach, your impact is now much, much bigger than a Yellow Pages ad. Think of a website as a super-Yellow Pages ad with 100 times the results at one-tenth of the price.

Stop waiting for customers to arrive or the phone to ring

It's scary to stand behind the counter of your shop with not a customer in view, or sit behind your desk with no incoming calls. It creates feelings of frustration, agitation, anxiety: unhealthy feelings that can lead to depression if not rapidly staunched.

So what do you do?

You can't force customers to visit you or cause the phone to ring – but you can take some practical action nevertheless.

Exchange offline inertia for online activity

Switch on your computer, go online, and engage in proactive marketing. It won't fill your cash register or your order book, but it will stop you feeling maudlin and outflanked by adverse conditions offline.

YOU NEED JUST TWO THINGS TO MAKE ONLINE MARKETING WORK FOR YOU

- Knowledge;

- Application.

This book will provide you with the knowledge, strategies, tools and techniques; the application is all down to you.

2
Why even the most unlikely small enterprises can prosper online

When your business is rapidly turning into a lemon as is the case with the unfortunate Oswaldtwistle storekeeper we met in the previous chapter, you are left with only one option; *make lemonade*.

On the face of it, this business would appear to be doomed; only a matter of time before the shutters are pulled down permanently and the enterprise consigned to the scrap heap. We see it all the time; small businesses going to the wall all around us. And yet, incredibly, for every small enterprise that closes down another one pops up in its place; the embryonic start-up syndrome in action. This must tell us something. It must indicate that regardless of adverse trading conditions in any given field, the entrepreneurial spirit of the small operator is far from snuffed out; it is alive and kicking as is evidenced by the encouragement provided to mini start-ups by central and local government alike; grants, low-cost loans, training, etc.

But there is another form of help readily available to struggling small enterprises: *self help*; and it is to self help that the Oswaldtwistle storekeeper should be looking, not just to survive but to prosper.

USING SELF-HELP TO ALLEVIATE DIRE CIRCUMSTANCES

Our hypothetical, under-pressure storekeeper (let's call him Ossie) must base his 'lemonade-making' strategy exclusively around the creation of incremental income from the surest source of revenue he will ever have: *the existing customer base*. Whatever is done by way of resuscitating this ailing business will have no impact whatsoever on the surrounding multiples although it could conceivably attract some additional custom from nearby competitive independents.

That, however, is not the purpose of the proposed online marketing exercise; the focus is on engendering loyalty and persuading existing customers to open their purses wider and spend more with their friendly grocer cum newsagent cum whatever else.

GETTING RID OF THE NEGATIVES BEFORE TACKLING THE POSITIVES

- "I don't have a computer and there is no cash available to invest in one."

Visit any computer superstore and acquire a brand new internet-connected machine at no deposit and with up to 12 months before a penny is paid out. Even then, if there is still no cash available, ownership can be obtained on deferred payment terms and the cost offset against operational expenses.

- "I can't afford the time or money to learn how to use a computer."

Nowadays that is not a genuine reason for failing to get up to speed on information technology; visit the nearest local small business initiative, community centre or public library and sign up for free evening classes on mastering computer basics. Children can do it, and so too can any business owner.

- "I don't see how a computer can help me increase my turnover."

Read on and find out how ...

GOING ONLINE: FIRST TO SURVIVE, THEN TO GROW

So what now for our theoretical storekeeper? Ossie has lots to do, but has made a good start already. He shopped around judiciously and settled on a package deal; the computer of his choice together with combined printer/scanner/copier and digital camera as free add-ons. He has also attended some evening classes and is getting to grips with information technology and how to handle the equipment.

Much of what lies ahead of Ossie initially is *offline* activity which is right and proper because his objective is an increase on instore sales as opposed to virtual transactions. These may come later, if at all.

OSSIE'S INTERNET CHALLENGE

- Ossie is about to use the world's most sophisticated and powerful marketing device to promote a corner shop but that's okay;

- His little mini-site will be in competition for the attention of internet users in tandem with billions of other web pages and that's still okay;

- Ossie has no digital products available for download, so even if he attracts a handful of visitors from outside his catchment area, he has nothing to sell them – and even that's okay.

OSSIE'S ONLINE ACTIVITY

1. He signs up with thirdsphere.com for online hosting and the service automatically generates his domain name (http://ossies-stores.com) and provides him with a web-based email facility.

2. He uses the system's point-and-click tools to build his small business mini-website.

3. The idiot-proof software makes it simple for him to create the page formatting described in Chapter 1: mission statement and complementary graphics on the home page (he uses the digital

camera to produce a product-pack image, scans and resizes it to fit); appropriate content for a supplementary page devoted to produce, sales and service; a third page inviting visitors to provide their email address and subscribe to his forthcoming newsletter. He also adds a link to this invitation to the first two pages.

4. Ossie defers inclusion of a 'Useful Tips' section until a later date but does include a *digital discount voucher* on his home page.

5. He has managed to accomplish all of this much more quickly than he had imagined thanks to the assistance he received from the system's 'Help' sector.

OSSIE'S CORE OBJECTIVE

The sole objective of http://ossies-stores.com to drive internet users from around the immediate neighbourhood to his virtual shrine and hence to his store – the only way he will drum up sufficient interest is to promote his new venture *offline* and locally.

WHAT OSSIE DOES OFFLINE TO PROMOTE HIS ONLINE MARKETING

Ossie will now use his newly acquired printer/scanner/copier to create the fodder for his offline onslaught.

1. He designs and prints out a window banner, section by section, which simply reads, "www.ossies-stores.com".

2. He prints out a quantity of pocket-size cards bearing the same message accompanied by appropriate sales copy; he hands a card to every customer who enters the store or he packs it in with the purchase.

3. He scans, copies and prints out a blow-up of the discount voucher featured on his website; it offers a 50 per cent discount on the advertised price of a merchandise line he picked up for

peanuts at a surplus stocks auction.

4. He sets up a mini-stall in a prominent position in his little shop. It consists of a table with an open ledger and pen, a barrel full of apples, and a card which reads,

> **WRITE DOWN YOUR EMAIL ADDRESS BEFORE YOU LEAVE AND HELP YOURSELF TO AN APPLE**

Not everyone has an email address yet but you might be surprised to discover how many do and just love to spread it around.

5. He produces 1,000 copies of a 2-colour flyer promoting his website and hand delivers these with the help of his family around the houses surrounding the shop.

6. He writes some basic text and produces a dozen or so mini-posters which he pins up with permission at the local lending library, post office, community hall, church entrance, etc.

7. He even talks a screen-printer friend into producing two transfers for his URL which he affixes on either side of the rickety old van he uses for visiting the local cash-and-carry.

Ossie will do more in time to promote his new venture both offline and online but this will be enough to get him started on internet marketing for his small business. He can never compete with the supermarkets and Oswaldtwistle Mills will forever be a thorn in his flesh, but what he can do is hang on to what he has, foster loyalty among his customers, and entice them to spend a little more on every visit. Goodwill engendered in this way has an age-old habit of generating referrals over time in the shape of new customers.

2 – WHY EVEN THE MOST UNLIKELY SMALL ENTERPRISE CAN PROSPER ONLINE / 15

REAL LIFE CASE STUDY

- Do you think all of this is a fanciful notion?

- Do you doubt it would work out in real life?

You should talk to my local corner shop owner. What you have just read is the strategy he employed at my suggestion to pick up a struggling store by the bootstraps and convert it into a thriving small business. Using the gift in the barrel ruse he picks up email addresses by the bucket load producing for him prospects that represent hard cash. My corner shop friend always uses apples for his gift, but it could equally be oranges or sweets.

1. His ruse works because he is giving something away for nothing and in return collects tangible assets for a pittance;

2. His list of subscribers is currently in excess of 1,000 and he emails them every week with news of special offers and discounted lines;

3. His website now provides visitors with an online ordering service for non-comestibles;

4. His store footfall has increased appreciably since he went online;

5. His average transactions have increased in value;

6. His fascia has been completely refurbished to incorporate a gleaming URL thanks to sponsorship from the local newspaper;

7. His small business now has a resale value substantially higher than it was before he discovered the dynamic of online marketing.

Internet marketing provides him with an interactive online presence which works for *any type of small enterprise*; even the most unlikely of propositions. And you don't even need commercial premises to make it work. You can use the dynamic anywhere, as I do; from the workstation in my living room overlooking the village green on frequent occasions …

3
Why the internet is tailor-made for small business

Just a few years ago it wasn't all that easy for small business to make its mark in the internet marketplace. Everything seemed to be geared to the big boys. Not any more: there is a palace revolution afoot and the beneficiary is small business. Microsoft, Netscape, Google, Yahoo!, Hotmail, BT, AOL, *et al* are all pulling out the stops to entice small businesses of every description into online marketing. There are new strategies, new products and new software streaming out of each of them which are specifically designed to assist the small entrepreneur (and I do mean *small*, with a staff of between one and ten) to get a firm foothold on the internet. Visit the website of any of these major online players, scan the menu of services, and you will see what I'm talking about.

Listed below are good reasons why the internet is now tailor-made for small enterprise but they barely scratch the surface of its potential for people like you and me. You know your own business, your product or service, your market, your niche and your customers. Put your thinking cap on and I'll bet you come up with a few more.

21 GOOD REASONS TO GROW YOUR SMALL ENTERPRISE WITH ONLINE MARKETING

1. Low start-up costs

Just a few pounds monthly for hosting fees, the purchase of a few pieces of essential software – which you might well pick up for free if you search around hard enough using the sources listed in this book –

and you're up and running. Compare that with the start-up costs of the average offline marketing programme.

2. Low maintenance: cost-wise and time-wise

Just a few hours a week should suffice in most instances and the tools you will need are all available for free. You will spot them and sources for downloading as you read the chapters to follow.

3. Heighten awareness for your small business

Creating a presence online is fast, and increasing awareness of your small business operation is equally rapid. Can you imagine what it would cost *offline* to achieve the same depth of recognition?

4. Improve your image

Whatever the nature of your enterprise and whatever the image you present offline, online promotion will add a touch of glitz that marks you out as a 21st Century marketer.

5. Stay local or go global

You will continue to enjoy all the advantages of an internet presence if you decide to restrict yourself to online marketing for local purposes, but you have the option to go global if you decide to engage in digitally-generated produce – there's more about this in the next chapter.

6. 24/7 trading 52 weeks a year

The internet never stops, not even for a breather; you will be trading around the clock, all 365 days.

7. Create incremental income from existing customers

This will be your prime objective if you stay local and an added bonus if you go global.

8. Attract new customers

Either way you will attract new custom in due course because online marketing is 'viral' in nature inasmuch as it replicates itself many times over – as you will discover in later chapters.

9. Grow your business exponentially

How rapidly you do that will depend entirely on how sincerely you commit yourself to mastering the principles contained in this book and how diligently you apply them to your own business and your own particular circumstances.

10. Become an expert in your niche

That is one of the wonders of marketing online; you can actually become and be recognised as an expert in your own niche – and just how you accomplish that is revealed in Chapter 5.

11. Sell digitally-generated produce

It's not nearly as difficult as you might think right now and in Chapter 19 you will discover if you qualify and how to go about it if you do.

12. Use digital discount vouchers for products and services

You have already had an example of how this works in practice and it will work for you too, if you exercise imagination and creativity in the construction of your discounted offerings.

13. Expand your market

As you become more and more proficient in online marketing techniques not only will your existing market increase in size, but you will also discover opportunities to move into new markets.

14. Deliver improved customer service

With powerful electronic tools at your command you will now provide your customers with better, faster, more sophisticated levels of service.

15. Foster customer loyalty

Now you will be able to get closer to your customers, cosset them, spoil them on occasion, and reap the dividends of your most priceless asset: *consumer loyalty*.

16. Research your competition

No more looking over your shoulder in the offline world. If they have websites, you can visit them, scrutinise what they're getting up to – and pinch some of their best ideas …

17. Source new merchandise lines

The internet is awash with valuable up-to-the-minute information on merchandise, deals and special discounts – even on a local basis.

18. Source new suppliers

If you are unhappy with current supply sources the internet provides you with *carte blanche* on locating alternative providers.

19. Keep up to date with market trends

What's in today is out tomorrow in many trades. Keep tabs online on what's happening offline.

20. Offer online ordering service

Offer your customers the option of buying online. Chapter 29 shows you how.

21. Collect subscriptions and create future customers

Can you think of a better, faster, cheaper way to build a list of targeted prospects? Chapter 24 will show you how to do it.

WHY YOU STILL NEED A WEBSITE EVEN IF YOU DO ALL YOUR BUSINESS OFFLINE

You currently do all your business offline and you're doing very nicely, but you still need a website …

Why? Just this:

- If you choose to ignore the potential of online marketing you are also choosing to miss out on a valuable extension to your existing customer base;
- What's more, you are also missing out on the opportunity of getting *closer* to your current clientele.

You might think that the internet, and more specifically your own little website, offers few opportunities for businesses with a customer base clustered in a small geographic area. After all, the Web is worldwide, a global medium. And you would have been fairly correct up until recently. But matters have been changing rapidly. More and more, *your* potential clients are forsaking those heavy Yellow Pages paper books for Google and other search engines. It's easier and faster to do an internet search when you need to find a supplier in a hurry.

WHY THE INTERNET IS SUCH A DYNAMIC MARKETING TOOL

We all know the Web is a resource for fun and information, but have you ever stopped to really think about its potential for dynamic marketing? If you already use a website to market your business, or are considering doing so, the following concepts may give you something new to consider.

1. A website is a fun and creative way to express yourself

The idea of online marketing seems to make many of us a bit uncomfortable. Using a website as a marketing tool is a way of having fun and getting creative in the process.

2. Anyone can have a website

Financially speaking, the Web is 'The Great Equaliser' of the marketing world. Whereas other forms of advertising and marketing, such as television, radio, and print media, are prohibitively expensive for small business concerns, anyone can use the Web to advertise and market their products or services for free. While the cost of creating a website may vary (based on size, the nature and amount of graphic design used and the experience level of the designer), the cost of running or maintaining a site over time is minimal as compared with other media. It is a means of advertising that is financially within reach of everyone.

3. Your website is a direct reflection of *you*

As the owner of your own website you control the message and the image you want to portray. You get to decide what you want to say – it's your own personal billboard. You have as much space to get your message across as you need, so use it well. Make it attractive, professional and functional, make it well organised, and make sure the *real you* is reflected on the screen.

Imagine you are a potential customer visiting your site for the first time.

- As a new client, what are you looking for?
- How easy is it to find pertinent information about you and your business?
- What's in it for the client?
- Why should they not only do business with you but repeatedly

visit your site to enhance their experience of your product or services?

> **TIP**
>
> Think about websites you've visited that you either loved or hated – and why – and apply those standards to your own site.

4. This is one time where it's considered okay to be 'work in progress'

With the Web you're virtually unlimited (pun intended). You can change it as often as you see fit – and frequent website updates are in fact highly desirable. The fresher and more innovative the content, the more valuable it will be to others. It is critical that you periodically review your site to see if it's getting stale and outdated and that you use it to keep your target market informed.

> **TIP**
>
> Even if your site is more or less under construction, dump those 'under construction' messages or graphics – a good site is always work in progress, and using those messages marks you as an amateur.

5. You'll have room to experiment freely – the Web is a very forgiving medium of self-expression

The great thing about the internet is that by its very nature it is intended to be changeable and flexible. Don't worry about getting it perfect or that you are locked into a design or look.

4
How to convert your local business into a global concern

By its very nature the internet dynamic fuses cultural links worldwide. Take China for example; it is just catching on to the internet, but imagine what will happen when the Chinese nation becomes fully connected. The already substantial global online market will double in size – and so it goes on; ever evolving, ever expanding.

Not every small business will be able to take advantage of these developments – our Oswaldtwistle storekeeper won't – but perhaps you can and here is how ...

BENEFITING FROM THE GLOBAL DUAL KNOCK-ON EFFECT

While I was writing my first published work way back in 1994 I was also engaging in the early stages of online marketing. I suspected that the book might have a positive knock-on effect on my online activity. I was right. But little did I realise it would turn out to be a *dual* effect; the book selling offline *and* online and in turn promoting my internet-generated produce.

I enjoyed the dual benefits when I started out, and so can you, and you won't need to have a book published to participate. Online marketing will increase your local trading offline and have the potential to present a global dimension online.

HERE'S HOW TO DETERMINE WHETHER YOU QUALIFY

1. Do you have an intellectual property or properties?

2. Would you allocate time to confirm what you *think* you know?

3. Would you undertake research to add to what you know?

4. Would you be prepared to learn how to digitise intellectual properties?

5. Would you get up to speed on promoting digital produce?

6. Would you investigate online payment and distribution facilities?

EVALUATING INTELLECTUAL PROPERTIES FOR ONLINE ADAPTATION

The majority of service-based small business operations are usually hinged on at least one intellectual property. It might be the service itself, the particular niche into which it fits in the marketplace, an exclusive slant the owner has developed for it, an elite customer assistance package, or all manner of other possibilities. Certain small manufacturing units have similar opportunities for digital application by way of exclusive documentation.

For example, one such concern might produce a tangible product in common use with multiple supply sources, universal demand and distribution, but for which the owner has discovered a use that no one else has yet tapped into. They all soon will of course, but the one who jumps in first usually holds on to that position for a time at least.

To evaluate the suitability for online adaptation of a formula or solution in both instances, the intellectual property must be evaluated for …

1. Conversion into a form of words in the shape of a digital product;

2. Conversion into a piece of electronic software.

If it scores on either count and is capable of attracting consumer demand outside the current trading area, the property is a prime candidate for online distribution.

CONFIRMING WHAT YOU THINK YOU KNOW ABOUT YOUR INTELLECTUAL PROPERTY

So far so good, but no one knows *everything* about anything. Your formula, your solution, your whatever, might be impeccable in your eyes, but ...

- Will it measure up to every requirement of potential future markets?

- Might it need some tweaking?

- Might it need updating?

- Might it even be flawed in some respects?

Go online, do some essential research, confirm what you think you know about your intellectual property and make adjustments if required. Better to do it now. It will be too late if you leave it until after you start production and online distribution.

USING ONLINE RESEARCH TO ADD TO YOUR KNOWLEDGE

Similarly, as you are using online research to confirm what you think you know, you can be adding to your knowledge. Seek out professional articles on the product, the market, consumer trends, pricing, etc.

CONVERTING INTELLECTUAL PROPERTIES INTO DIGITAL PRODUCTS

Many small business owners already marketing online shy away from the subject of digital conversion in the mistaken belief that the process is difficult, time-consuming and expensive. Nothing could be further from the truth; it is simplicity itself. There are truckloads of help available on digital conversion of intellectual properties – online and in Chapter 19 of this book. I have hundreds of digital products circulating around the internet; ebooks and software covering a complete spectrum of specialist interests, by far the majority of which I make available as free downloads (you'll discover why in Chapter 11) but when I started out I had no idea what a computer chip was and I still don't know.

As long as you take the trouble to learn *why* digital conversion works, it doesn't matter that you don't know how.

PROMOTING DIGITAL PRODUCE

Mastering the digital conversion process takes you halfway; the other half consists of becoming skilled in the art of promoting your produce online. These arts are explored in the following chapters:

1. Marketing in the correct niche (Chapter 9).
2. Choosing your domain name (Chapter 10).
3. Building websites (Chapter 11).
4. Creating content-rich pages (Chapter 12).
5. The power of 'keywords' (Chapter 14).
6. Search engine positioning (Chapter 15).
7. Flooding your site with low and no-cost traffic (Chapter 18).
8. Analysing your online footfall (Chapter 32).
9. Email marketing (Chapter 22).

10. Using articles to lure visitors to your site (Chapter 20).

11. Publishing your own newsletter (Chapter 23).

12. Building a list to assemble a bank of prospects (Chapter 24).

13. Linking to other websites (Chapter 21).

14. Converting virtual prospects into real customers (Chapter 28).

15. Getting it all together for maximum impact (Chapter 36).

ACCEPTING CREDIT CARD PAYMENTS ONLINE

Unlike me, you will no doubt want to *sell* most, if not all, of your digital produce and to do that successfully you need to know how to accept credit payments and organise online distribution (Chapter 29).

Go global if you can and watch your small offline business operation zoom to new and higher levels of profitability online.

5

The power of recognition as an expert in your niche

Few people go online specifically to purchase products or services; believing that they do is the biggest mistake that most marketers make. People use the internet to track down *information* about products, services, whatever; information that leads them to a solution; a solution to a problem they are currently experiencing. When you grasp this indisputable fact you are in a position to enjoy the unique power of being recognised as an expert in your own niche – and the internet makes it easy for you because all the information people are looking for is categorised in precise cubbyholes.

IMPARTING INFORMATION THAT PROVIDES SOLUTIONS

The power of being recognised as an expert in a niche is personified in the article below published in a national daily newspaper on 7 September 2005.

- *The information sought*: finding lost friends;

- *The solution*: wrap every conceivable eventuality in the website database.

LET'S BE FRIENDS
Website set for £120m sale

FRIENDS Reunited is in takeover talks which could spark a £40,000,000 windfall for founders Steve and Julie Pankhurst.

The website which helps old pals get back in touch is being sized up by several big media and internet rivals.

And a bumper £120m bid for the business, set up just five years ago, could be just weeks away.

News of the talks came as the founding couple celebrated their seventh wedding anniversary in Cambridge.

Boss Michael Murphy said: 'We can confirm that the firm have recently received a number of credible approaches.'

The Pankhursts set up the website with long-time friend Jason Porter during the dot.com boom. Steve, 41, only agreed to launch the site after a string of other business ideas failed.

More than 12,000,000 have now registered their details online and profits this year should hit £6.5 million.

The site has rekindled friendships, helped lovers track down old flames and been blamed for Britain's rising divorce rate. The Pankhursts originally ran the site from their semi-detached home in Barnet, north London, while looking after their first daughter Amber.

They brought in Murphy, a former Financial Times executive, two years ago when their second child Sally was born.

He now handles the day-to-day management of the company alongside a team of 50 staff in Oxted, Surrey.

The Pankhursts still own a third of the shares.

Experts believe broadcasters ITV and Channel 4 or magazine publisher EMAP could make a move.

Friends Reunited have already bought recruitment site Top Dog Jobs.

Steve and Julie did it their way with incredible results but you can also achieve the power of recognition as an expert in your niche doing it your way. While it is highly unlikely you will emulate their success, you might just do enough to put your small business on the map – online.

WHY EXPERT STATUS IS MORE ATTAINABLE ONLINE THAN OFFLINE

This power is formidable and it is yours to command whether you decide to remain local or convert your business into a global concern. What's more, you can attain expert status much quicker, more easily, and less expensively online than were you to attempt to do so offline. You will be using the incredible muscle of the internet to make your mark and you will have at your disposal the world's most sophisticated tools – and all at no charge.

THE TOOLS YOU WILL NEED TO MARK YOURSELF AS AN EXPERT IN YOUR NICHE

The tools you will need are the very devices you will use to promote your business online and the simple secret to marketing yourself as an expert in your niche is *the care you will take* in presenting the information you wish to impart.

This information must:

- provide genuine solutions;
- be reliable;
- herald you as someone who knows their business;
- breed trust;
- cause people to regard you as an expert in your field.

It is not enough to give the impression that you are an expert; you must *prove* it in all that you claim your information will accomplish.

POWERING UP THE TOOLS WITH YOUR EXPERTISE

- **Your website** is your virtual storefront and sales pitch rolled into one. No matter how modest the format, make sure the presentation is professional. You don't need lots of images and gismos; it is words that matter, words that convey your philosophy, carry authority, instill confidence in the reader that you know what you are about; words that not only indicate but prove your expertise.

- **Your articles** are a prime vehicle for demonstrating your expertise online and you should be churning them out at regular intervals, distributing them at least once a month to the ezine directories listed in Chapter 20. Never treat article writing as a boring chore. Embrace it with passion. It has the power to brand you as a connoisseur faster than any other activity you will undertake online. Conversely, treat article writing with disdain and you will be branded as an amateur. The screen capture immediately below provides evidence that anyone can achieve expert author status for their article output.

- **Your newsletter** is equally important in building your reputation online because when subscribers opt to join your list they have a right to expect quality, eloquence, and factual information in every communication you send out. Provide them with anything less than total commitment and they will drift away in droves faster than it took you to enlist them.

- **Your email marketing** must be charged with the same dedication because despite the difficulties currently experienced by marketers using this medium it still exercises tremendous influence on your status in the marketplace.

- **Your links to other websites** should always be chosen with extreme care. Link to the wrong sites and people will get the wrong impression about you, your business and your standing as an authority in your niche.

PROVIDING SOLUTIONS TO PROBLEMS

The power of recognition as an expert is not the exclusive province of big business. You can acquire expert status for a small business niche with a mini-site providing the information you purvey provides users with genuine solutions to problems.

It could even make you famous ...

6
How to become famous online as a small business owner

I'd run a mile if anyone ever offered me a system on how to become famous offline, but I am very happy to have my name, mug shot, articles and output plastered across thousands upon thousands of other people's websites.

ONLINE FAME PROMOTES YOUR PRODUCE AND ITS 'SECRECY' KEEPS YOU SECURE

• Becoming famous online is neither overt nor in-your-face recognition.

• No one is going to stop you in the street, ask for your autograph, pester you or text you with dumb messages.

• No one in your circle will ever know you are famous unless you tell them.

Online fame is *private recognition* that has incredible power; the power to fulfil your ambitions and help your small business grow dynamically if you use it wisely.

It is not difficult to achieve – when you know how – and you will know how by the time you have completed your first reading of this book. I say 'first' because you would do well to read it a second time or at least cherry pick some core chapters. As you are learning how to become famous online as a small business owner, you will also be absorbing a whole host of strategies; essential strategies such as ...

HOW TO CAPITALISE ON THE AMAZING POWER OF YOUR OWN NAME

Turning your own name to your advantage online hinges on linking it to a series of proactive measures in logical and progressive sequence; measures you will master as you travel through the pages of this manual. It won't come easy; there is work to be done – but it will be worth it when you see your name up in virtual lights without spending a penny – and better still – when your name fame bounces back onto your small business operation.

This technique is more powerful than you think

Your success will be multiplied many times over when your name is easily recognised and people in your particular marketplace feel they 'know' you. Similarly it becomes easier to network, make money, and receive privileges once your name gets around.

It is the law of association at work

When you are well known, you must be 'good', and when you are famous, people will want to be around you because it makes them look good too.

HOW TO WRITE ARTICLES THAT SIZZLE, TRIGGER SALES, AND INCREASE YOUR ONLINE FAME

Let's start where we mean to finish – at the top – and our first port of call is your own particular expertise. Linking that special knowledge to the amazing power of your name represents the second secret to becoming famous online ...

You are a walking compendium of learned life skills: work, hobbies, general interests, specialist interests, child bearing/raising/educating, and so on. The list is endless. In one of these areas you are an expert and the chances are high that your own special expertise lies in what you do for a living; your intellectual property; your small business operation.

Chapter 20 will show you how to write dynamic, high-quality articles tagged to your name; articles that will spread your fame online and trigger sales for your business. You will get the hang of it very quickly and when you do, you will be churning out one or two articles at a time, quite effortlessly.

HOW TO SWAMP THE WEB WITH YOUR ARTICLES

You will learn how to swamp the Web with your articles and increase your online recognition at zero cost. What's more I will provide you with my private list of the top 30 article submission centres; hubs that have my own articles circulating daily on tens of thousands of other people's websites; hubs that will do just the same for your small business.

HOW TO TURN YOUR ARTICLES INTO TOP GRADE PRESS RELEASES

Chapter 20 will also instruct you on how to take your articles and convert them seamlessly into top grade press releases; how and where to send them – and all for free.

HOW TO INCREASE YOUR FAME THROUGH THE POWER OF LINKING

Another clever zero cost way of getting your message across is through the power of linking to other sites (Chapter 21); not any old sites, but sites specifically related to your topic. Take the trouble to sniff them out by undertaking some basic research.

HOW TO SNARE THE 'SPIDERS' AND GENERATE TOP TEN RANKINGS ON DEMAND

The 'spiders' are the electronic robots dispatched by all search engines to assess your website for keywords, content and links value; the stuff that determines where, if at all, your site will be positioned in the listings. Chapters 12, 14 and 15 cover these elements in detail but in Chapter 16 you will be provided with an exclusive tool to ensure that your website is always positioned in the top ten rankings.

Here is just one example of what you can achieve with the tool I am going to give you free of charge ...

Your eyes do not deceive you. This website hit the No.1 spot in its genre on Yahoo! out of **1,830,000,000** competitive pages (yes, one **billion**, 830 **million**). What I achieved, so too can you for your own small business site if you follow the simple instructions that accompany the tool.

HOW TO PRODUCE A NEWSLETTER THAT STANDS OUT A MILE

When you start a newsletter focused on your small business operation you are embarking on a very exciting and rewarding venture – watching your online publication grow, trying out new tactics to attract subscribers, even making some money. It becomes addictive. You'll see why as you progress and Chapter 23 will show you how to get started.

HOW TO GET PROSPECTS QUEUING UP IN DROVES TO SUBSCRIBE

Driving subscriptions and enhancing the profile of your newsletter are core activities for success in online marketing. There are 300,000 other newsletters competing for the same subscribers so the better you become at chasing your goals, the faster you will succeed. Gaining momentum is the hardest part. Where do you begin in your quest for say, 10,000 subscribers and maximum exposure? Chapter 23 reveals the answer.

HOW TO GIVE STUFF AWAY FOR FREE AND GALVANISE YOUR ONLINE FAME

I set up a website http://free-stuff-xl.com offering $370 (approx. £200) worth of my own personally-generated produce to every new subscriber to my newsletter. Did my experiment work? You bet it did.

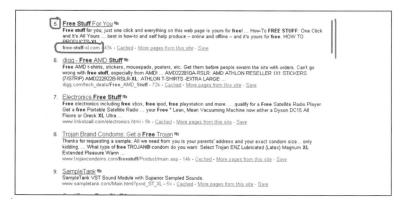

Within hours of submission of the URL this site rocketed to Rank No.5

out of 143,000,000 competitive web pages with corresponding high rankings in all of the other major search engines. Chapter 30 shows you how to find stuff to give away – and it won't cost you a penny.

HOW TO CHANNEL YOUR ONLINE FAME INTO OFFLINE ACTIVITY

As your online fame grows it opens the doors to opportunities offline; opportunities to enhance your reputation and create strings of incremental income. Chapter 35 tells you how.

These are just ten of the techniques you can use to become famous online. Couple them with the strategies you will absorb through the remaining chapters and you will have at your command a formidable arsenal which you can use to make the most dynamic marketing device of the 21st Century *really* work for your small business operation.

Meanwhile, how about this as an example of the power of the online fame game …

REVEALING THE HIDDEN POWER OF ONLINE FAME

We all know you can learn more about any topic online but do you also know that you can find out just about anything about anyone *who is anyone online* and yet not invade their privacy; film and TV personalities, sports stars, politicians – even small business owners. Do you find it hard to believe that little fish swimming in a big pond can rise to the top? Then using me as bait, look at the screen capture opposite; you are presented with lots of information about lots of people bearing the name 'Jim Green' but right up there at the very top of the first page, just above the 1st out of **30,000,000** page references and again twice to the right, you will find stuff about me personally.

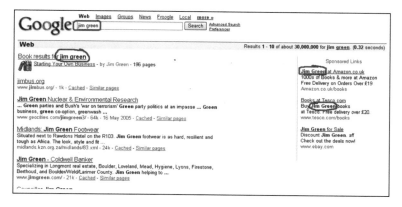

- How do you do that?

- How do you get your name flagged *before* the official listings?

- How can it help your small business grow?

I could give you several other examples using different strategies – but I will do better than that. Visit the site below. It promotes a digital product which I created; an innovation that shows you how it's done and introduces you to a myriad of ways to become famous online. But don't buy the product at this website. Just read about it and then email me jimgreen@writing-for-profit.com with 'Famous' in the subject line and I'll get right back to you with the link where you can download it for free with my compliments.

http://howtobecomefamousonline.howtoproducts-xl.com

7
Creating your plan of action for the internet

Rushing around willy-nilly to find success online will get you nowhere. No matter how hard you try you won't find it that way, but do all the right things in the right order and *success will find you*. To start the process you need a plan, a plan of action for your small business online marketing adventure.

WORDS OF CAUTION BEFORE YOU START ON YOUR PLAN

Make sure it's your plan and yours alone; you will find all you need for its formation right here in the pages of this book. Above all, avoid like the plague the peddlers of high-priced counsel; counselling on affiliate programs, ezines, email marketing, linking strategies, joint ventures, search engine optimisation, meta tags, keywords, Google, Overture, pay-per-click, pay-per-impression, FFA Sites, link farms, reciprocal linking strategies, safe lists, opt-in lists, double opt-in lists, RSS, blogging, copywriting, tools to do this, tools to do that, files for this, binders for that...

It is all frippery and fandango; all for show and not for blow; over-priced and worthless for the most part. Give these shameless hawkers the slightest sniff and they will fleece you. Keep your plan simple and structured to the precise requirements of your small business operation, refraining from *ad hoc* inclusion of snippets you pick up for free along the way and most particularly those tidbits offered by the cowboy counsellors.

And if you must pay for advice on any issue, make certain in advance that it comes from a trusted source before you part with your hard-earned cash.

STICK WITH THE PLAN; DON'T CHOP AND CHANGE

The second biggest mistake that most marketers make is to chop and change before they give their plan a chance to work. Do your thinking and research beforehand and stick with the strategies you choose to run with. No one becomes a successful online marketer overnight: it takes time, patience and dedication.

QUESTIONS YOU WILL WANT TO ASK OF YOURSELF

1. What is my mission?
2. Will I stay local?
3. Will I go global?
4. Which type of website will I need?
5. What about a domain name?
6. What sort of offline activity will I engage in to promote my site?
7. How much should I set aside for start-up costs?
8. How should I budget my time?
9. Is my core aim incremental income?
10. Do I want to expand in other areas?
11. Will I use the internet to freshen up my image?
12. How important to me is acquiring expert status in my niche?
13. Will I engage in marketing digital produce?
14. Will I be using electronically-generated vouchers?
15. Will I use the internet to deliver superior customer service?

16. Will I use it to foster loyalty among my existing clientele?

17. Will I set in motion an online system for monitoring my competition?

18. Will I be sourcing new merchandise online?

19. Will I use online research to track market trends?

20. Will I use it to source new or additional suppliers?

21. Will I be offering an online ordering service?

22. Will I set up a free newsletter and solicit subscriptions?

There will be other questions you will want to add to this list and only you can come up with the answers; answers that will add flesh to the bones of your plan.

MISSION STATEMENT

To kick start your plan you'll want to compose a brief statement of your overall aims in engaging in online marketing. Keep it brief; a paragraph or two at most should suffice. Use it as a constant reminder of why you are doing this and to ensure that you are focused on achieving the targets you set yourself.

STAYING LOCAL OR GOING GLOBAL

Clearly if your business is strictly local in nature like a neighbourhood store, garage or window cleaning service you won't be going global. Think seriously, though, before ditching the global route if your area of operation is more flexible and capable of expansion: the internet offers inexpensive avenues of reach that are unavailable offline.

YOUR WEBSITE

The type of business you operate and how adventurous you intend to be in your marketing will determine the type of website you require. In the majority of cases a simple 2–3 page mini-format should be adequate, but if you surround yourself with a battery of promotional tools from the arsenal you will be reading about shortly then you ought to consider a multi-page approach from the outset.

YOUR DOMAIN NAME

The domain you choose *must* reflect the character of your enterprise and you will learn why in Chapter 10.

PROMOTING YOUR WEBSITE ONLINE AND OFFLINE

You have a plethora of alternatives at your disposal, offline and online. We looked at some of the former in an earlier chapter and the entire range of online promotional options is discussed in detail in the chapters to follow.

START-UP COSTS

Apart from website hosting your start-up costs should be minimal. You will find in the pages of this book (and repeated again in the Resources section) online sources where you can download for free most of the basic tools, but you should make a contingency for the few you will need to purchase.

BUDGETING TIME FOR SERVICING THE SITE

One of the prime benefits of marketing online is the time-saving factor. Once you are underway, by far the majority of essential daily tasks are performed automatically. Regular manual servicing such as submitting your site to the search engines, checking on the functionality of links, etc, adds next to no time to your working schedule.

DELIVERING SUPERIOR CUSTOMER SERVICE ONLINE

Now you can move up a few notches on the customer servicing scale. Chapter 33 shows you how – and why you will miss out if you fail to take advantage of the electronic assistance your website is geared to provide.

FOSTERING LOYALTY AMONG YOUR EXISTING CLIENTELE

Get your existing clientele to subscribe to your newsletter and email them regularly with special offers, discounts, loyalty bonuses and the like. Keep in touch, keep them informed, and they will keep coming back for more.

MONITORING THE COMPETITION

Now more easily and effortlessly than ever before you are in a position to keep tabs on competitive marketing, pricing, promotions. Even if some of your competition is not online yet, you can still keep tabs. The search engines don't need permission; they gobble up information– even from the most unlikely quarters.

SOURCING NEW MERCHANDISE

Expand your merchandise range; add new lines, and all at a few clicks of the mouse button.

SOURCING NEW SUPPLIERS

Finding new supply sources is easier and quicker online – even for the smallest of enterprises.

TRACKING MARKET TRENDS ONLINE

All of us involved in small business must have a finger consistently poised on the pulse of ever-changing market trends; there is no faster device than online research – and it's free.

DELIVERING AN ONLINE ORDERING SERVICE

The nature of your small enterprise will decide whether or not this is feasible. If it is, Chapter 29 directs you on how to go about matters.

SETTING UP YOUR NEWSLETTER

Don't hang about – skip ahead to Chapter 23 and make a start now …

And now in Chapters 8 to 36 we will review in depth the strategies and tools you will need to enact your internet plan of action. Do not treat any of this as an exercise simply to be seen to be 'doing something' online. That would be a complete waste of your time and energy and accomplish nothing. Proceed rather with total commitment on your decision to engage in online marketing to grow your small business rapidly.

8
Why marketing online is fast, easy and stress-free

A fairly common reason given by small business marketers for just 'doing something' online is the time factor. Rather than take full advantage of the tools at their command they settle for a meagre internet presence under the mistaken impression that total commitment would inflict even greater pressure on their already stressed work schedule. Nothing could be further from the truth. Online marketing is fast, easy and stress-free because, for the most part, it is automatic. Even so you will still need to embark on a prescribed learning curve and that's what the next 28 chapters are all about. And, when you are through with your studies, your virtual store can be any size you like – as big as a mall or as small as a market stall – with no limit on the amount of products you can offer.

10 INBUILT ADVANTAGES TO MARKETING SMALL BUSINESS ONLINE

1. Minimal start-up costs.

2. Work your own hours.

3. 24-hour trading.

4. Open 365 days a year.

5. Marketplace: the Planet Earth.

6. Level playing field, even if your website consists of a solitary page.

7. Automatic order taking.

8. Automatic payment processing.

9. Instant shopper satisfaction.

10. No customer interfacing.

We haven't even scratched the surface but don't you already get the feeling that the online route sounds faster, easier and less stressful?

CUTTING YOUR START-UP COSTS TO THE BONE

You can start your online marketing for next to nothing even when you trade in digitised merchandise. Apart from your domain name (and these come dirt cheap nowadays) your only other basic start-up costs comprise page creation tools and website hosting, but I'll show you in Chapter 11 how to obtain all three in a unique piece of software that offers a great deal more besides. I'll also direct you in Chapter 19 to another software tool that will produce your initial e-produce for free.

CHOOSE YOUR OWN HOURS

There is no requirement for you to be strapped to your computer because, as you will discover as you progress in your studies, almost *everything* connected with the enterprise can be set to automatic pilot. You can be totally flexible, going about your offline duties as normal and choosing your own hours for attending to online marketing.

AROUND THE CLOCK ORDER-TAKING

Automation can be positioned to accept orders electronically every second of every day and every night. We'll examine your options in Chapter 26 where I will also let you in on my favourite order-taking software; how it works; how inexpensive it is to operate – and why it is the perfect solution for the small business owner who elects to deal in digitised produce.

THE INTERNET IGNORES PUBLIC HOLIDAYS AND NEVER TAKES A HOLIDAY

It can't help it. The internet is always open; it doesn't even close down for a quick breather. It ignores public holidays and it never takes a holiday.

- Can you imagine the scope this unique marketing opportunity presents for the dedicated small business owner?

- Can you envisage how vast the internet marketplace will become when within the next few years the 55 million existing customer base will be extended by many millions more as Asian users kick in?

- Can you think of any offline business that is faster, easier and less stressful?

- Can you see now why so many small businesses are missing out by continuing to settle for a mere presence online?

It gets even better when you learn how to combine both online and offline in promoting your ideas. I'll show you how I do it in a later chapter.

HOW YOUR LOCAL VIRTUAL STORE REACHES OUT INTERNATIONALLY

The local store housed in your computer is contained in a microchip measuring less than half the size of a postage stamp and yet it has the power to reach across the globe and do business internationally. You can't see how this would be of much use to you? Then allow me to illustrate from my own experience. Eighteen months ago I launched an information product that was intended for local writing groups. What do I find a year and a half on? 92 per cent of downloads are from the

USA, 7 per cent from the European Union, and only 1 per cent from the UK. You may discover something similar when you start doing business online- especially if you function in the service sector.

YOU WILL BE MANAGING YOUR ONLINE AFFAIRS ON A LEVEL PLAYING FIELD

Providing the virtual stall you set up is of the highest standards (and there is no problem in attaining these) then you will be competing on equal terms with the major players. The computer operating your little online empire could be housed in the front office or the back of the shop but no one will ever know. That's the beauty of online trading: *anonymity*. It provides a level playing field for everyone and no one can steal a march on you because by the time you have finished reading this book you will know how to access the same marketing tools the moguls use – and they will work for you even if your site consists of a solitary sales page.

THE CHOICES OPEN TO POTENTIAL ONLINE CUSTOMERS

When people visit your website and review your produce or service they make one of four decisions:

1. They buy on the spot;
2. They decide to move on and find something better, cheaper – or free;
3. They decide to come back again later for a second look;
4. They decide they're not interested.

When they decide to buy digital produce on the spot (or return later to buy) they want the merchandise immediately and they want it without any hassle. With automatic ordering they can have what they want because the entire transaction takes only seconds. Even if you deal in tangible goods you still score with automation; the deal is sealed, the sale confirmed, and the cash rung up on your virtual till.

VIRTUAL TRANSACTIONS GET THE CASH IN FAST

Virtual transactions get the cash in fast because the process is fully automatic:

- Customer produces credit card details online;
- Transaction is authorised;
- Sale receipts are deposited in your virtual account.

You will need a facility to accept credit cards because without one you will miss out on 90 per cent of the potential sales for your e-produce. I will give the two best options in Chapter 29.

ONLINE IT'S WIN-WIN ALL ROUND

The customer gets the produce, you get the cash; you both get what you want. A bond is created and in retail parlance that equals goodwill. How you use it is your business, but you would do well to nurture its power.

CUSTOMER SATISFACTION RESULTS IN ADDITIONAL SALES

The most productive avenue for future sales will always remain the list of customers who previously bought from you and were happy with the purchase. The potential here for additional sales far outstrips any programme you might put in place to attract new business.

WHY VIRTUAL CUSTOMER INTERFACING CUTS DOWN ON STRESS

In an offline business, customer interfacing can prove arduous. It is ongoing and covers issues such as product information, demonstration, general enquiries, and complaints. Virtual interfacing eliminates the stress. Answers or directions covering most customer issues can be hosted in a web page devoted to **Frequently Asked Questions** (FAQ).

9
Why niche marketing works best for small business

Whatever the nature of your enterprise it is almost certain that you operate in a precise niche and this is good news because exact positioning in the internet bazaar is where online marketing works best for small business.

Billions of services and products are sold on the internet, so you want to identify a niche that allows you to position your business in a positive way to an existing, receptive market – and the best way to identify a profitable niche is to *find an unfulfilled want; then fill it.* Even if tens of thousands of others in your industry understand your area of expertise, perhaps you have a unique spin, slant or twist that will make your offering stand out and shine above the others.

WHAT YOU MUST DO BEFORE YOU START

- Identify your niche market;

- Identify your niche customers;

- Identify the produce or service the niche market and its customers want.

DON'T TRY TO SELL EVERYTHING TO EVERYONE

The cardinal sin the major players were guilty of in the spectacular crash of a few years back was that they all set out to sell everything to everyone; everything they thought that everyone *needed*. Their profligacy cost them and their backers millions upon millions of pounds. It cost them dearly because they considered niche markets too small, too insignificant, too expensive to reach, and too slow to develop in the reckless drive for immediate returns to match their massive investment. They were wrong in every way; they paid the price; they bombed.

DON'T RISK FAILURE BEFORE YOU START

It's sad, but even today the vast majority of online businesses still manage to fail before they actually begin because 98 per cent of them don't know how to go about choosing a niche.

They make one or other of two huge mistakes:

- **Mistake no. 1 – Targeting a market that is too broad**
  (e.g. Trying to compete with Amazon.com by selling books or other common household items online)
- **Mistake no. 2 – Targeting a niche that is overly saturated**
  (e.g. Trying to get a foothold in the 'Internet Marketing' or 'How To Make Money Online' niche)

INFORMATION OUTSTRIPS ALL OTHER E-COMMERCE NICHE PURCHASING OPTIONS

This list says it all …

Top 5 e-commerce niche purchasing categories

a) Computers (4.3 million buyers);
b) Electronics (7.4 million buyers);
c) Software (9.6 million buyers);
d) CDs/Videos/DVDs (11.2 million buyers);
e) Digitised Books and Information (**17.5 million** buyers).

Information products outstrip all other e-commerce niche purchasing options and this opens the door to you in the development of your own online marketing plan. The list, incidentally, is extracted from a Forrester Survey (the internet research arm) of online buying patterns for the year 2004.

THE SECRET OF SUCCESS

The secret to long-term success online is to position your strategy in tiny – but popular – niche markets that have little or no direct competition, and then create and sell digitised information products to these niches.

PEOPLE BUY WHAT THEY WANT, NOT WHAT THEY NEED

That's it then in a nutshell. When people go online to buy, they buy what they *want*; not what they necessarily need or what other people say is good for them. Allow me to illustrate with a true story that dates back long before we had colour television, mobile phones, or the internet.

HOW NICHE NOUS SUSTAINED A 50-YEAR CAREER FOR A FAMOUS BANDLEADER

The famous bandleader Joe Loss was a master at finding out what his niche customers wanted and as a result stayed at the top of his profession for over 50 years. When Joe and his orchestra played in provincial dance halls he invariably used his break time for market research. While the band members sloped off for a beer, Joe mingled with the patrons enquiring after their *current* tastes in popular music. He did so because he never took for granted that what was hip today would necessarily be so tomorrow. Joe always had his finger on the pulse of cyclical change and frequently bucked the trends that other bandleaders followed unremittingly in the mistaken belief that they knew which musical styles dancers *needed*.

Joe knew his niche market inside out, knew his customers, and always knew how to give them exactly what they wanted. He knew because he *asked* them, and so too can you ask your customers, not face to face but virtually, as you will discover.

HOW TO SPOT YOUR OWN EASY-TO-TARGET NICHE MARKET

Don't treat the following tasks lightly; think seriously about them and go beyond the obvious. Many opportunities and breakthroughs lie in the final stretch. In other words, expand your mind, because the best ideas will probably be found further down the list past the first more obvious ones. You will never know until you test.

1. Think hard about what would constitute your ideal niche.
2. Jot down every possible use for your product or service.
3. Come up with a series of keywords or keyword phrases that accurately reflect these areas of usage.
4. Now produce a separate list of the words your *customers* might use in a search engine to identify these uses.
5. Compare your lists and select the strongest keywords and keyword phrases.
6. Choose the top five and endeavour to match them with profit centres for your product or service.

Now take the core words from your narrowed-down list of keywords and profit centres; type them into a few major search engines; investigate each item on your list.

• Do you see a pattern emerging?

• Can you find websites, newsgroups and newsletters that focus on your findings?

- Do these findings coincide with a *prime niche market*?

- How large and identifiable is the niche?

- Who is the competition?

- What do they do?

- What are they selling?

- What are their target markets?

- How are they positioned?

- What's missing?

- What problem can you perceive that is not being currently addressed?

- Could you provide a solution?

- Could you come up with a product or service that the niche wants and will buy?

To achieve this latter objective, frequent the newsgroups, forums and discussion groups related to your niche. Look at the questions being posted daily. Talk to the participants. Ask questions. This is how to determine what potential niche customers want, not necessarily need.

I engaged in all of the foregoing before I set about identifying the niche for my own first online product and just look where it ranks now:

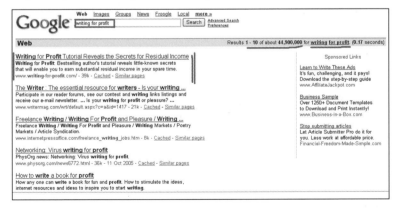

DEVELOPING A PRODUCT OR SERVICE THAT PROVIDES A SOLUTION

By now you should have identified one or two easy-to-target markets and, if you have done your research properly, you have probably also identified a problem the target market is currently experiencing. If you haven't found one yet, keep looking. It may take a little more time. If people are asking questions on newsgroups, forums, discussion groups that you do not understand, contact them individually and request clarification. Keep going until you uncover a problem, a want, a need.

Now brainstorm again.

- What types of produce or service can you develop to help solve the identified problem?

- More importantly, determine whether your solution will sell.

Once you have defined a solution, ascertain if your identified niche market is willing to part with hard cash to own your prescribed answer to the problem. Always remember, a recognised need does not necessarily translate into sales. Just because someone apparently needs something it does not mean that they will *want* it badly enough to splash out cash. If your target audience is unwilling to purchase your product or service for whatever reason, or if you have identified more problems than you can solve, discard the market and move on to the next one. Never get hung up on trying to flog a dead horse.

Nonetheless, the most profitable products are those you can develop yourself, because that way you control the costs. But you may have neither the skills nor the resources to achieve this. If that is the case, look around for a joint partner who *already has the solution* but is not doing a very good job of marketing it. Make an offer – and be sure to put it in writing. You'll never know if you don't ask.

Throughout the entire process of finding a product or service that people want, bear in mind that while almost anything sells over the internet, you should focus on produce that can be digitised and easily automated. Become 'auto-pilot' minded. This will allow you to expand into several profitable online pursuits that combine to create multiple income streams.

Above all – think niche.

TESTING THE POTENTIAL FOR YOUR NICHE MARKET

You will begin by using the search engines to gauge the popularity of keywords and key phrases related to your particular niche. The number of sites displayed for, say, the keyword 'swimwear' will provide a notional indication of the overall niche market size. But that is not enough. Now you need to establish how many times per month 'swimwear' is being searched for by users. When you've found that out, you can also determine the keyword's popularity – i.e. the number of times the term is searched for as opposed to sites available for scrutiny.

- **Are there more sites than users searching for the keyword?**
  If there are, you've just found an oversaturated niche, so drop it.

- **Are there more users than sites available for searching?**
  Then you've located an under-worked niche, so go for it.

FREE SOFTWARE THAT SUPPLIES THE ANSWERS

Here is an exceptional tool that will provide the answers in relation to every niche keyword you can come up with. You may use it free of charge.

Good Keywords – Measures everything from keyword popularity to a website's popularity and beyond. Download the software at this site: www.goodkeywords.com.

You've located the perfect keyword(s) for your perfect niche, but now you want to find out more about your market.

Here's what to do. Go to www.google.com and undertake a search for 'niche articles' (replacing the word 'niche' with the *root word* relating to your niche). You will be presented with hundreds (if not thousands) of highly informative free articles.

HOW YOU CAN TELL IF YOU'VE STRUCK IT NICHE

1. You have located an easy-to-target niche market.
2. It is easy for you and other people to identify.
3. You know where to reach your perfect customers.
4. There are sufficient numbers of them.
5. There are newsgroups they frequent.
6. There are websites they visit.
7. There are newsletters they subscribe to.
8. You have identified a problem this niche market is currently experiencing.
9. You have developed a product or service to provide a solution.
10. It's something your potential niche customers want, not need.
11. You have tested the market and now know they will buy from you.

DEVELOPING THE SALES PROCESS FOR YOUR NICHE MARKETING

The next step in the formula is arguably the most challenging. The difficulty lies not in the principle, but in its application; knowing what works in online promotion and what does not. So vital is this challenge that the remainder of the book is devoted to its exposition:

- Finding a great website name;
- Registering your website address as your trading name;
- Developing a compelling sales message;

- Obtaining the required e-commerce services;
- Developing systems for the fulfilment of your orders;
- Developing sound customer service strategies;
- Capturing visitor names and email addresses;
- Remaining in contact with both customers and website visitors;
- Designing, optimising, uploading your website;
- Developing strategies to attract online buyers ...
  - search engines
  - newsletters
  - classified ads
  - banner ads
  - affiliate reselling
  - article submissions
  - linking strategies
  - web page content
  - online publicity
  - offline publicity.

SECRETS TO UNLOCKING CORE NICHE FACTORS

You will find them all in Niche Factors: a special report that will cost me $27 (approx. £15) but you can have it for free by sending a blank email to jimgreen@writing-for-profit.com with 'NICHE FACTORS' in the subject box.

Now let's move on to the vital matter of publicising your produce, because if you are not prepared to learn how to promote effectively, you might as well stop reading right now ...

10
Why your domain name must reflect your enterprise

There's a lot in a name; more so when it's a trading name; even more again when you are using it to market your small business online.

THE CATALYST THAT DRIVES THE ENGINE

Your domain name is the catalyst that drives the engine containing all the other factors that combine to create high ranking spots in the major search engines – and you will discover why when you arrive at Chapter 16.

Above all, the domain must accurately reflect your product or service and, if in the process it breaks some (or all) of the conventional rules in devising a trading name for offline application, so be it.

Your marketplace is cyberspace and if you have to cut a few corners to come up with the name you want to run with – then cut them.

I use names online that I wouldn't dare to use for my offline ventures; names such as:

- 1st creative writing course;
- how to products xl;
- making money online;
- costcutters;
- madhatter;
- how to become famous online;

- website optimisation;
- start a business masterplan;
- free stuff xl;
- retirement moneymakers.

Ten ugly, cumbersome, tongue-twisters if applied offline; ten winners when used online ...

FITNESS FOR PURPOSE

It's a question of fitness for purpose; they all tie in exactly to the respective produce I am promoting, that is they accurately reflect the product or service.

Let's dissect the reasoning behind four of these ugly bugs.

Why '1st' creative writing course?

Because someone had already registered http://creative-writing-course.com and also because ...

(a) '1st' indicates superiority;

(b) Some search engines (like Yahoo!) list numerically prefixed URLs before alphabetical prefixes.

Why 'xl'?

Same reason: http://howtoproducts.com and http://free-stuff.com had already been registered – plus the fact that 'xl' can also mean 'excel' ...

Why 'costcutters'?

Because prices are cut to the bone on all the produce featured on this website ...

Why 'retirement moneymakers'?

Because what I am promoting here is a course directed at retirees on how to make money online in their spare time …

NO FINESSE REQUIRED

Straightforward, down-the-middle, to the point; but then, I am not chasing literary prizes, just enticing the 'spiders', the robotic dirt devils that determine where (if at all) websites are positioned in the search engine listings.

Whichever route you take in choosing your trading name, make sure it's your name and not some concoction based on a free hosting service domain, like for example http://howtoproducts-xl.freeservers.com. All that will get you is the bottom of the pile.

EXCEPTION TO THE RULE

Paradoxically, though, you *can* get away with such cheese-paring when you tag the trading name to an existing URL that you registered yourself … and you use the unique system revealed in Chapter 16.

For example, http://howtobecomefamousonline.howtoproducts-xl.com ranks No.1 on Yahoo!, AltaVista and AllTheWeb.

DO'S AND DON'TS FOR CHOOSING YOUR OWN DOMAIN NAME

So, now that you are convinced that you need your own domain, how should you name it? Here are a few do's and don'ts; try to follow as many as possible.

1. **Consider naming your company and registering a domain name starting with the digit 1.** Better still choose a name starting with '1st'. Why? When people create directories of websites they have to decide how they are going to classify the submissions. One way to classify sites is to list them on the basis of how 'good' they are. Another way is to simply list them in chronological order (and sometimes in reverse chronological order) based on the dates the sites were submitted.

    The other – and far more popular – classification system is alphabetic. Now, the first character in the ASCII chart which can be used as the first character in a domain name is the digit 0. The next character is the digit 1. Normally, you wouldn't want to start a domain name with the digit 0 since it might send out all the wrong signals to your customers. Instead name your domains starting with the digit 1. More specifically, name your domains starting with '1st' (for example http://1st-creative-writing-course.com). This will ensure that you get a high alphabetical placement in those directories which classify sites alphabetically. Furthermore, depending on the niche market in which your pursuit operates, it may also send the right message across to your customers –indicating that you are the first venture to consider in the niche.

    And guess what – the mother of all directories – Yahoo! – lists websites alphabetically based on the *title* that had been submitted. Yahoo wants the title to be the official name of the site. This implies that sites which start with the digit 1 will be placed at or near the top of a category. **That's why http://1st-creative-writing-course.com features in the Top 10 on Yahoo! out of 8,000,000+ competitive sites.** Assuming that you can get your site listed in Yahoo!, just consider what a top ranking in one of the categories in the directory can do for its popularity.

Furthermore, a small caveat here. If you are going to name a domain starting with '1st', also register the domain which starts with 'ist'. Then, have the domain containing the vowel 'i' redirect visitors to the domain containing the digit 1. This is because people will often type in 'ist' when they mean '1st' and vice versa. Also, for every email alias that you create for the domain containing '1st' (like sales@1stcompany.com), you should create the corresponding email alias for the domain containing 'ist' (like sales@istcompany.com). Incidentally, this strategy is especially significant in the case of registering a domain for a new venture.

2. **Don't want to start your domain name with '1st'?** Consider starting it with 'A', 'B' or 'C'. Although domains starting with A, B or C will be listed after those starting with the 10 digits, you can still get a pretty high alphabetical placement.

3. **Try to register a domain which contains a popular keyword applicable for your niche.** This will help your customers remember your domain name better. Furthermore, for searches conducted in Yahoo!, a higher ranking will be given to those websites which contain the keywords in the title. And according to Yahoo!' instructions, the Title should always be the official name of the site. Thus, if the domain name contains a keyword, you will be able to include the keyword in the title which will improve your ranking. As a minor side benefit, this can also help to increase the ranking of your website in some search engines. Hence, in an ideal case, you should register a domain of the form 1st [keyword].com (without the brackets of course).

4. **Don't register a domain containing the digit 0** in it, unless it is going to be part of a recognisable word (like 1000 or 2000). This is because the digit 0 is often confused with the vowel O. If you feel that you must register a domain with the digit 0, make sure that you also register the corresponding domain containing the vowel O.

5. **Try to avoid using domains that contain '2' for 'To', '4' for 'For', 'u' for 'You'** and so on, even if they seem to make your domain sound 'cool'. Your customers will easily get confused if you do so. However, if you must register such a domain, register the expanded form of the domain as well, i.e. if you are registering www.greatthings2do.com, also register www.greatthingstodo.com.

6. **Should you or should you not use hyphens in your domain**? Well, the jury is out on the question. While some internet marketers will tell you that domains containing hyphens are difficult to remember, spell and pronounce, others will state that they are, in fact, easy to remember, spell and pronounce. The controversy surrounding hyphens didn't bother me when I registered www.writing-for-profit.com. Personally, I would consider that whether or not hyphens are helpful has to be determined on a case-by-case basis. However, if you register a domain containing hyphens, make sure that you also register the corresponding domain without the hyphens. Once you do that, you can simply redirect visitors from the domain without the hyphens to the domain with the hyphens.

7. **Don't make your primary domain too long.** Even though 67 character domains are a reality, exactly how many of your users will want to type a domain name like www.thisisanexampleofaverylargedomainname.com?

8. **Always use '.com'.** Avoid using domains ending in 'nu' or 'to'. Your venture will have little credibility if you do. You can consider registering a '.net' domain, but since most people are more familiar with '.com', it is better to stick to convention. Alternatively, if you intend to limit your online marketing to a strictly local basis, choose 'co.uk'.

While it is unlikely that you will be able to register a domain which satisfies all the rules that I outlined above, try to follow as many of themes you can.

TIP

Visit www.1stSearchRanking.com where you can invest in their service promising top placement in all of the search engines or your money back. Alternatively, consider using either of the website hosting services featured in the next chapter. Both do it all for you automatically.

11
Building a website tailored to your precise needs

Having chosen a domain name that reflects the nature of your enterprise, the next task is to create a website tailored to your precise needs as a small business owner. Thereafter, everything else you do must mirror the image of the virtual identity you are creating block by block in logical progressive sequence.

MINI- V. MAXI-WEBSITES

There's a lot of be said in favour of both, but for niche markets and niche produce (which is where you ought to be focusing your energies) it is best to opt for mini-sites: one, two or three page websites. Read on and I'll give you several sound reasons why.

Maxi- or multi-page sites on the other hand are more practical where you have lots of information to impart before you can interest prospects sufficiently to make a purchase or to instruct them where you are offering training services. I use both options where applicable and for the purposes just stated.

THE PERFECT VEHICLE FOR SMALL BUSINESS ONLINE MARKETING

The mini-site approach is perfect for niche produce such as stand-alone ebooks and software because it provides a simple one-shot vehicle: a sales letter coupled with an online order form. You will almost certainly be starting out with a single product or service in your initial foray into internet marketing, so a well-constructed mini-site such as I am about to illustrate will suffice. Later, when you are up and running with several propositions in tandem, you might well consider switching to the multi-dimensional approach.

Mini-sites will work for you providing you have:

• Identified your niche market;

• Found out where your niche customers hang out;

• Mastered the art of creating a compelling sales letter;

• Learned how to build a one-shot marketing site;

• Learned how to promote it effectively.

SALES LETTERS STYLED IN THE ADVERTORIAL FORMAT

The best and most successful mini-sites aren't designed as in-your-face billboard advertisements. Certainly they are sales letters, but presented in a format that resembles the advertorial style we are all familiar with as we browse through magazines. They are informative and more often than not, touchy-feely. They set up the stall, identify a problem or highlight a want, promise a solution, make a spiel, elaborate on the benefits, and wind up with a pitch for the sale.

THE APPROACH ISN'T NEW; IT HAS BEEN WORKED SUCCESSFULLY FOR OVER 200 YEARS

Recall just a few years back when hardly a week went by without at least one 4/6/8-page promotional piece in the shape of a sales letter popping through your mail flap. Mini-sites are the virtual equivalent. The approach isn't new; it has been working successfully offline for more than 200 years. You may even have used it yourself if you operate within the service sector.

HOW TO CREATE THE COMPONENTS FOR YOUR VIRTUAL SALES LETTER

1. **The header graphic block** – This is an illustrative visual that announces the title of the produce. It works best when there is a hint of colour, and it could contain a picture. It can also be a generic block covering multiple produce such as one I use myself: *FreeStuff*.

2. **The headline promise** – Comprises a few pithy words that highlight the major benefit you are offering: the solution to an identified problem.

3. **The testimonials/credential block** – Here is where you lay out your credentials for creating the product and reproduce one or two testimonials. You won't have any from paying customers yet, but what you do instead is pass the product around friends and colleagues to elicit some glowing reviews.

4. **The product introduction block** – Introduce your proposition as the solution to a given problem and include a graphic in the shape of a digitally generated ebook cover (see Chapter 19 for the ideal software).

5. **The benefits block** – Bullet-point all of the produce benefits (not the features). This will more readily assist readers to visualise how the problem will vanish when they own the product.

6. **The guarantee block** – Don't be shy about offering a watertight guarantee. This is how to convert procrastinators and stave off refund requests.

7. **The call-to-action summary block** – Make it positive, make it compelling, make it bullish; make it easy to buy, make your prospects reach out for their credit cards.

THE ALL-IN-ONE SOLUTION FOR
DEVISING MINI-SITES

Here is the best tool on the market for constructing mini-sites. It does everything automatically to ensure that your site is a winner:

- Designs the header block;

- Writes the sales letter (yes, you read correctly, it *actually* writes your pitch): follow the promptings of the software, answer a few questions, follow the directions, and watch your sales letter take shape;

- Creates the mini-site.

This amazing all-in-one software costs $97 (approx. £53) and is available for download at www.saleslettergenerator.com.

THE PERFECT WEB HOSTING SERVICE
FOR MINI-SITES

This is the unique service you read about in the opening chapter:

http://thirdspherehosting.com/plus/?xstcreat&id=xstcreat&pkg=

Flip back to Chapter 1 now and refresh your memory on the gist.

Perhaps most important of all: it provides you with the ability to create and market *unlimited numbers of mini-sites* with separate directories but all under the *same* domain. What a saving. It works like this: you register a niche domain name, say, http://howtoproducts-xl.com. Then, using Third Sphere hosting you simply create a sub-domain http://articles.howtoproducts-xl.com and so on for as many separate associated e-products as you like. I use this service myself and consider it a bargain at $25 (approx. £13.50) per month.

WHEN YOU NEED TO USE THE MULTI-PAGE APPROACH

My own website www.writing-for-profit.com uses the multi-dimensional approach because it has many functions to perform. It markets a comprehensive tutorial on the topic of writing niche non-fiction; it dispenses free ebooks and complimentary reports on the subject; it provides instruction on e-writing; it contains a massive resources directory; it test markets disparate digitised produce, etc. And it also gives away completely free of charge reams of valuable information.

Why does it do all this?

Not to sell the tutorial; that's incidental. It does it all to sell more of my published hard copy titles in worldwide bookstores and online at Amazon.com.

That is why I use the multi-dimensional approach. You will have another reason when you come to consider it: multiple produce.

THE CUTTING-EDGE TOOL THAT DOES IT ALL AUTOMATICALLY

If you were forever manually to operate all of the mandatory chores we will be discussing in future chapters you'd drive yourself nuts and, what's more, have no time left over to accomplish what you really set out to achieve: *grow your small business rapidly online*. Fortunately, that need not be the case. You have at your disposal a cutting edge tool to do it all for you automatically when you operate a multi-page website – but not before you've cut your teeth on the basics of manual operation. Why? Because only when you know 'how' can you appreciate 'why'.

THE WAY TO CREATE AND MANAGE A MULTI-PAGE WEBSITE

What you need to make the most of the e-commerce experience is software that frees up time to enable you to concentrate on the primary function: marketing your venture. Such all-embracing software is available to you and it is proving a popular route with many small business entrepreneurs because it is less demanding and permits one-to-one virtual interfacing with potential customers. Should this be of interest to you (and it's worth investigating) you might consider investing in the all-in-one tool that I use. It will set you back $499 (approx. £273) annually but what you receive for your money is awesome. Site Build It! is available for immediate download at http://buildit.sitesell.com/interactive1.html.

WHAT YOU GET FOR YOUR INVESTMENT

1. Domain name registration.
2. Hosting.
3. Power keyword research, analysis and implementation.
4. Graphic tools.
5. Point & Click page building.
6. Choice of page templates.
7. FTP to upload your files to server.
8. Form builder/Auto-responder.
9. Data transfer.
10. Email.
11. Newsletter publishing facility.
12. Brainstorming & researching for the right keywords.
13. Spam check.

14. Daily traffic stats & click analysis.

15. Search engine optimisation.

16. Automatic search-engine submission.

17. Automatic search-engine tracking.

18. Automatic search-engine ranking.

19. Pay-per-click research & mass-bidding.

20. Four individual traffic headquarters.

21. Action guide & fast track guide.

22. Integrated online help.

23. Express ezine to keep you up to date on new developments.

24. Tips & techniques.

25. Customer support.

26. Facility for uploading/downloading digitised data.

The Site Build It! Traffic Center outstrips by far all other alternatives I have so far encountered. Once you have the hang of it (and that doesn't take long) you just sit back, leave it all to the software as you watch your traffic soar day by day.

It's awesome!

12
Creating content-rich pages to lure the 'spiders'

There is an old saying, 'a picture paints a thousand words'. Not so online. Words rule, words are king. Apart from your header and product blocks, only add pictures and graphics if you are convinced they enhance and support your copy. That way you will see that most of the beautifully designed logos, banners and gizmos you had in mind will simply distract the 'spiders' (and your visitors) from the most important thing on your site – your sales message.

Now let's explore each task in turn ...

• Creating content-rich pages;

• Interlacing them with keywords.

SO YOU RECKON ALL THIS IS BEYOND YOU?

Perhaps you're trying to write web copy for the first time. Perhaps you don't even consider yourself a writer. Perhaps you think it's too late to start now.

Wrong ...

You've been a creative writer all of your life; when you were composing essays at school; when you are writing business letters; when you put pen to paper to produce a reasoned argument why you have fallen behind in your VAT payments.

YOU ARE AN EXPERIENCED WRITER BUT YOU DON'T GIVE YOURSELF CREDIT FOR IT

This time you are charged with developing content for a topic you know a great deal about: *your own business*. You conceived it, you built it; you know more than you think you know; you are an experienced writer, but you don't give yourself credit for it. Writing about your business should be a pleasure, not a chore.

You just follow some basic rules and let it all hang out. Don't get all strung up; have some fun instead ...

TECHNIQUES THAT WORK OFFLINE WORK EQUALLY WELL ONLINE

There is no mystique. The techniques that work offline work equally well online. You will have to make some changes, of course, to accommodate the restrictions imposed by the computer screen and the problems that navigation sometimes presents. But the successful techniques for effective web copy remain the same. And these techniques have been around for centuries.

Good web copy doesn't attract the attention it deserves. Copy just isn't cool because well-crafted persuasive text doesn't attract attention to itself. It just sits there on the page delivering its message skilfully and unobtrusively; focusing attention on the product and the reader; quietly doing its job of selling.

And most of the really successful internet marketers employ excellent, *uncluttered copy* on their sites. That's why they are successful.

It's so easy and cheap to build a website these days and set up a storefront. And that's great. There's room for you and your online opportunity to compete alongside the big boys. And with no previous business or advertising experience you can build a 100 page super-duper animated site in minutes. But when the sales don't come in, the answer seems to be to change the animated GIFs, Java scripts, site banners and other gizmos to grab the attention.

Meanwhile the clever marketers, the successful ones, rake in the sales with strong, professionally crafted selling copy; copy they've taken the time to learn to write for themselves. They know it is words that sell, not gizmos. Which words?

Words that sell

After you have drawn up the approximate overall structure of your site, and before you design the fine details, decide what you're going to say and who you are going to say it to.

Now begin writing your copy

Write it, rewrite it and cut out the dead wood. Crystallise your message. Hone it, polish it, and examine every single word for relevancy and maximum effect. Keep rewriting it until you're sure it's a winner. Don't be tempted to 'make do'. If it takes a week and it's still not right – spend another week until it is right. And a third week if need be until you're absolutely convinced you can't improve another single word. Remember, it is your online opportunity that's at stake.

Here's an excellent tip

Print out your copy and read it out loud. If it doesn't sound like an everyday conversation, there's something wrong. Have a friend read it out to you. If he/she stumbles over any words, or has to reread a sentence, you'll know it needs rewriting.

Then build the website around your copy.

VITAL FACTORS THAT POINT THE WAY TO GOOD WEB WRITING

1. Far too many websites have no headline. If your web pages

haven't got headlines, you will lose out. Just because your reader is already at your page doesn't necessarily mean he knows what to expect. A headline tells him what to expect. It also gives you, your offer, and your site an identity that is, preferably, memorable.

2. Fire your biggest gun first – in your headline.

3. Push your USP into your reader's face.

4. Pack your message with benefits, benefits and more benefits.

5. Use plenty of white space.

6. Break your copy up into bite-sized chunks.

7. Make it easy to contact you from every page.

8. Place a 'Home' button on every page.

9. Make your copy as long as it needs to be to get the entire message across.

10. Emphasise your key points.

11. Use testimonials with imagination. Don't just list them on a separate page. Your readers won't look for them.

12. Give the reader a call to action (for example, 'Order Now!')

13. Make it extremely easy to order.

14. Show your reader how to order.

15. At the ordering stage restate your guarantee.

16. After your reader has submitted their order make sure they are told the order has been received. Then send them a Thank you email. They need to be reassured they have made the right decision. Prevent 'Buyer's Remorse' or they may cancel.

17. Be totally professional about absolutely everything.

ENCOURAGING INTERACTION WITH YOUR WEBSITE VISITORS

Try always to persuade the reader to become involved in the message you are putting across and you can do this by:

- Connecting with readers immediately;

- Capturing their attention;

- Holding their interest;

- Speaking to their concerns;

- Answering their unasked questions;

- Overcoming objections;

- Compelling action;

- Valuing their time.

So there you have it

A brief summary of the copywriting techniques used by the most successful marketers and copywriters on and off the web; just ordinary people with the good sense to stick to proven methods which achieve extraordinary results.

Great interactive writing is easy to read, but often hard to write.

Here's a closing thought from a master of words, Winston Churchill:

> *Had I had longer, it would have been shorter*

HOW TO LACE YOUR TEXT WITH KEYWORDS THAT ENTICE THE SPIDERS

It seems a shame to inflict your beautifully crafted web page copy with seemingly unrelated keywords and you may be tempted not to bother.

Resist the temptation

If you don't include them, your pages won't even be listed by the search engines let alone achieve top ranking positions. You see, while the spiders love rich content, they love judiciously sited keywords even more. Niche keywords are the bait that entices the spiders to rank your pages and position them accordingly – in the top spots.

However, be warned, do not overload your rich content with keywords; judicious placement is the operative term. Depending on the length of your page text, repeat your prime keyword *three to five times* (a dozen times or more if you decide to major on one keyword); for the others (you should use between six and eight supplementary words or phrases) *once or twice, but no more*.

The moral is …

- Content-rich pages with keywords get the top spots;
- Content-rich pages without keywords get ignored by the spiders.

TRY THIS EXERCISE IN KEYWORD SPOTTING

Below is the text from one of my prime web pages illustrated above.

- See how the copy flows naturally;

- See how the keywords gel;

- See how they don't distract the reader from the sales message;

- *See also if you can spot those keywords in the text …*

Exclusive New Website Optimisation Snares The Spiders And Generates Top 10 Rankings On Demand!

How to Seduce the Spiders Into Ranking Your Sites In the Top Spots – Exclusive

New Website Optimisation System Shows You How …

Yes, I know, you've heard it all before, but this exclusive new website optimisation system really does work and I will prove it to you if you read on.

Check out 12 real-life examples of its incredible power and then download the entire system on 60 days' evaluation so that you can test it out for yourself with your own websites, your own produce.

And no, this website optimisation system is not complicated.

1. You don't need to be a geek to make it work;

2. You don't need HTML expertise;

3. You don't need to master tricky codes;

4. You don't need to install any complex software.

You could be starting out today stringing together the pages of your very first project and you can still put the power of website optimisation to work for you with this unique system; effortlessly and passively.

And no, it is not expensive.

You could spend 1000s in subscription dollars on conventional website optimisation strategies and still end up drowning in the back end depths of millions of search engine pages for popular keywords. With this system you will get your share of the top spots at a miniscule fraction of the cost you would expect to pay.

Click on the links below for a dozen real-time examples of the consistent strike rate of this exclusive new website optimisation system.

It generates Top 10 Rankings on demand!

'This Unique Website Optimisation System

Captures Top 10 Rankings In The Major Search Engines!'

Click on the Links for Undisputed Proof of This Statement

- How to rocket a product website from nowhere to Rank Nos. 8 & 10 out of 725,000,000 competitive web pages on Yahoo! (Yes, you read correctly, seven hundred and twenty-five million) ZERO COST

- How to rank a top-selling product at No.1, 2, 3, 4, 5, 6, 7, 8, 9, 10 consecutively on the same high ranking Google page! ZERO COST

- How to zoom another product website to rank at No.2 out of 10,200,000 competitive web pages on Yahoo! ZERO COST

- How to rank a brand new product at No.1 on Yahoo!, AltaVista and AllTheWeb instantly! ZERO COST

- How to get another brand new product site to Rank No.17 out of 143,000,000 competitive web pages just 24 hours after submitting the URL to Yahoo! ZERO COST

- How to link to sought-after resources that direct prospects to your sales pitch! This page is No.2 out of 10,800,000 sites on Yahoo! ZERO COST

- How to have your own name ranking at No.1 out of 30,000,000 web pages on the Google world wide search engine ZERO COST

- How to repeat the process on all major search engines ZERO COST

- How to be acknowledged as an expert articles author ZERO COST

- How to dominate the top ezine hubs with your articles ZERO COST

- How to have the same hubs cascade your articles across millions of other people's web pages ZERO COST

- How to make miniscule changes to your articles, transcript the material into media releases and spread them like a virtual virus ZERO COST

You don't get major search engine rankings like these by chance nor do you get them by working your butt off into the wee small hours evolving individual website optimisation strategies.

You get them by using a unique straightforward all-in-one system that works first time every time irrespective of product or service and the ever-changing algorithms. It works because it always provides what the spiders love to see when they visit.

If you skipped those links scroll back and click on them now

So Who Needs Pay-For-Clicks?
You Can Do It Yourself For Nix!

I get thousands upon thousands of visitors to my websites every week and not a single one of them is activated by the pay-for-click services.

1. I have never invested a thin dime in them;

2. I don't use them at all;

3. I don't need them.

All of my traffic is generated by this unique website optimisation system and it comes from the most reliable source of all; the zero cost major search engines.

Stop throwing away your money; bin the pay-for-clicks and do it yourself for nix.

Revealed: The Core Keyword Strategy That Seduces The Spiders
And Captures Top Rankings

There is a knack; a little-known knack of deploying keywords and keyword phrases that represents the cornerstone of website optimisation. This secret strategy is revealed; stripped down in descriptive words and pictures to empower you to activate it within minutes on your own sites.

What You Will Discover In This
Unique Website Optimisation System ...

1. How to choose power keywords to dominate your niche

2. Where to locate the best free tools to tighten up your selection

3. How to position your keywords to snare the spiders

4. How to interlace web page copy with your chosen keywords

5. How to keep it flowing so only the spiders notice the keywords

6. How to seduce the spiders into fail-safe website optimisation

7. How to unravel the secret of strategic positioning

8. Why your domain name is germane to website optimisation

9. Why your index page heading plays a vital role in rankings

10. How to treat your site title tag to hit the high spots

11. What you must do to make your site description irresistible

12. How to start the keywords tag to ensure top rankings

13. What must always constitute the linchpin in your sales copy

14. What to do and what not to do when submitting URLs

15. Why the spiders love to visit when this system is in residence

16. Why this system works irrespective of ever-changing algorithms

17. How to get it all together to feature in the Top Ten

Why You Will Save A Fortune With This
Unique Website Optimisation System

You only pay once but you can hit the high spots forever after on all your sites with this unique website optimisation system.

- No monthly subscriptions;

- No calls on your credit card when you can least afford it;

- No further charges after a one-off payment.

*Would You Like To Seduce The Spiders Into
Ranking Your Sites In The Top Spots Using Real Website
Optimisation?*

At zero risk you can test out this unique system and make an early start on implementing its power-laden strategies at home for 60 days before you make your mind up on committing to full ownership.

- I take all the risks

- You get all the benefits

Spend 60 Days sampling and mastering my proven techniques and you will be unable to restrain yourself from committing to full ownership of this unique website optimisation system.

DID YOU SPOT THE KEYWORDS?

You probably clocked the first two but here is the complete list for your perusal – together with repetitions …

**Website optimisation: 21 times
How to: 23 times
Top 10: ranking 3 times
Search engine:7 times
Article 5 times
Keyword: 9 times**

You may be surprised that 'zero cost' doesn't figure as a keyword on this page. After all it is repeated 13 times in the text.

- It does not rate in this instance *because it bears no relevance to a product that is for sale*.

- It is included in the sales copy to highlight the fact that the entire system can be operated free of charge.

Despite what I have just said, the website ranks No.1 on several minor search engines for 'zero cost' …

So there you go; you just never know …

13
How to write sales copy that sizzles

You want your sales letters to be blockbusters, to sizzle like sausages in a frying pan; to attract cash paying customers. And so I am revealing in this brief chapter how I do it myself. Let's take as an example the copy for the sales pitch in one of my most successful mini-sites and dissect it to see what makes the text tick …

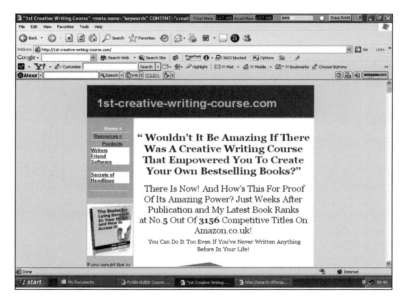

You can't tell much from the screen shot but when you've finished reading this section go to the site and you will see for yourself how the text not only incorporates the building blocks and the 17 vital guidelines, but also embellishes them. The subject matter in this instance is creative writing tuition, but it could be anything because if you follow the guidelines below your sales letter will sizzle, whatever the topic.

http://1st-creative-writing-course.com/bestsellers.html ranks at **No.17 out of 8,440,000** competitive pages on **Yahoo!** with its parent site featuring at **No. 14**.

FOLLOW THE GUIDELINES TO PRODUCE YOUR OWN SIZZLING SALES LETTERS

Visual Block

There it is right at the top and in this instance I replicate the URL because the headline and sub-headline immediately below are strong enough on their own to arrest immediate attention.

Headline

It's a grabber: addresses the market (writers) directly; poses an intriguing question; intimates that an answer is forthcoming.

Sub-headline

It provides not only the answer but also proof positive that it is a genuine answer that can be verified. In other words, Amazon.com rankings that browsers can check out for themselves.

Sub-sub headline

Reinforces the validity of the statements contained in both headline and sub-headline.

Product image

Strong, vibrant, professionally executed.

Introductory copy

Straight to the point, cuts straight to the chase, provides stimulus for the prospect to continue reading.

Examples

Practical proof that the product does what the copy claims: examples of author's produce and its sales rankings.

Testimonials

When you look at the web page you will see that I include not one but five testimonials. The moral: when you have them, use them.

Bullet point benefits

Scattered throughout in groups; the more the better.

Price justification

It's not enough to blandly state the price. Give justification, give reasons, elaborate on value.

Bonuses

I'm not offering any in this instance – but I tell prospects why.

Guarantee

You won't sell your products without one. As you can see I'm totally upfront here: unconditional, lasts for a lifetime ...

Call to action

You want the order? It's easy. Just *ask* for it.

Ways to pay

You must offer a credit card facility – but go one further as I do here – offer also PayPal or a similar payment processor.

Postscript

Always end your sales letters with a postscript – or better still two or three as I sometimes do. Make them clinchers. More often than not they push wavering prospects into reaching for their credit cards ...

So there you have it in a nutshell ...

Once you master the technique, you can do it over and over again for every product you develop.

Don't be fazed about composing your sales letters. Talk to prospects directly.

IMAGINE YOU ARE A MARKET TRADER ADDRESSING YOUR AUDIENCE

In fact, make a point of visiting a street market soon, listen to the traders making a pitch, observe how they ensnare the audience – and learn from them.

Do it this way – it works!

YOU CAN DEVELOP DOZENS OF PRODUCTS USING THIS CONCEPT

Can you really do this?

Produce dozens of products from one idea?

Yes, you can.

I've done it several times over – and I'm still doing it.

I first came across the technique many years ago after my very first hard copy bestseller was published.

It happened this way ...

Imagine the comparison between the contents list in a traditionally published book with the concept for a blockbusting sales letter.

They are both chock full of individual **benefits** (not features) that if dissected produce even more stand-alone product ideas.

So ...

- Looking at the contents list for my first book threw up several new ideas which in turn resulted in the subsequent publication of **6 new books** from the original bestseller.

- Looking at the blockbusting sales letter for my first online product ('Writing for Profit') motivated me to produce another **6 creative writing courses** from the same topic.

- Looking at the blockbusting sales letter for another online product ('Starting a Business Masterplan') resulted in yet another **6 ancillary guides**.

And I'm only just starting to milk this strategy ... I've got dozens more projects from a single idea lined up on the drawing board for execution in the years to come.

Does this concept work? You bet it does! There is a defined market for all of them because **perceived value** always lies in the eyes of the **individual** buyer. Now, it is highly unlikely that you will be promoting a creative writing course but that doesn't matter. Think about your own business, think about the service you offer, think about how you could divide it into stand alone sub-services.

TIP

Incorporate into your sales letters the simple guidelines I have provided and you will produce blockbusting sales letters that will attract, persuade, convince and convert casual browsers into cash paying customers.

14

Why power keywords are central to successful promotion

Target the wrong keywords for your small business website and all your efforts at snaring the spiders and dominating your niche will be in vain. Net result: you will lose out and you won't be making any money online.

WATCH YOUR TRAFFIC SKYROCKET WHEN YOU TARGET THE RIGHT KEYWORDS

Think long and hard about what keywords people are likely to use to find you. What words would *you* choose to search for your niche proposition? Make lists of keywords and then combine them into two or three word phrases.

For example, you rarely want to target a *single* keyword because with the billions of words indexed on the web right now, one keyword won't normally cut it on the average search.

People learn quickly that if they type in 'properties' they get listings for property from all over the world. It would be nice if your URL popped up there on those extremely broad keywords – but a better use of your time is to *pair* the generic keyword with something more specific. You might get lucky and rank well on just 'properties' as it is in your page but, if not, you'll probably end up at somewhere like 120,350 (or worse) in 'UK properties'.

Using *paired keywords* will also bring you far more qualified prospects for your product or service.

WHAT PEOPLE DO WHEN THEY DO A SEARCH ONLINE

Statistically, most people search with two to three word phrases to avoid getting back too many unrelated matches. Keep this in mind when you design your page(s).

Don't worry about there not being enough top ten slots where you can achieve a high ranking.

True, there are some keywords that are very competitive, especially in the realm of work at home, shop or office opportunities.

And if you find that no matter what you do, you can't get in that top ten spot for that word or phrase, just be creative. There are so many other keywords and keyword combinations where you can achieve a top ten ranking.

It's really not very difficult at all. Once you tap into some phrases people are searching on to find your type of website, you'll have tapped into a continuous stream of *free advertising* for your small business idea.

For example, if you don't achieve a good ranking on 'income idea', keep trying, but also be creative and target 'extra income idea' too.

THINK AS YOU THINK YOUR CUSTOMERS WOULD

It's all about thinking like your customer or clientele – and finding a keyword combination that can *dominate* in the search engines. You'll often find that there are more people searching for these other phrases than were searching for the first phrase you thought of. In marketing, this is called carving out your niche and when you are marketing your own small enterprise, isolating a unique niche in everything you do is central to success.

If you're Microsoft, you can afford to fight over who has the best 'browser software'. But, for the rest of us, we know we can't always fight the big boys. So instead, do what savvy marketers do: detect a niche that few others are targeting and go after it.

Good management is the key to achieving a range of good rankings, each of which will bring you scores of new visitors – if you choose the proper keywords.

WHAT ARE PEOPLE SEARCHING FOR?

You need to know how many people are searching for one keyword over another. 'Search volume' is the number of times a specific keyword is searched over a period of time.

Having knowledge of search volumes will give you a sense for what is being searched for and what keywords you may want to focus on. Good places to look up search volumes are suggestion tools like these – available at zero cost.

http://inventory.overture.com/d/searchinventory/suggestion/

www.wordtracker.com

www.adwordanalyzer.com

You will need to conduct market research to decide on which keywords to focus on. Keep in mind that the more popular keywords are competing for the top listings – some are searched for several thousand times more than others.

So the keywords you use to pull in customers may vary accordingly. The goal is to find keywords or keyword phrases that fetch up a good number of searches, but do not have as much competition.

More on this vital topic a few paragraphs on ...

WHY HOMING IN ON NICHE KEYWORDS PRODUCES INSTANT RESULTS

Here is a practical illustration from my own experience.

I spent a considerable amount of time researching before targeting niche keywords and keyword phrases for this particular website but the effort was worthwhile because it brought me instant results in that the spiders loved what they saw and ranked it accordingly: No.1 out of **1.9 billion pages on Yahoo!** (yes, 1,900,000,000) plus eight top ten rankings on the other major search engines. What I have achieved, so too will you for your own small business site if you follow to the instructions in this chapter – and in Chapter 16 to follow …

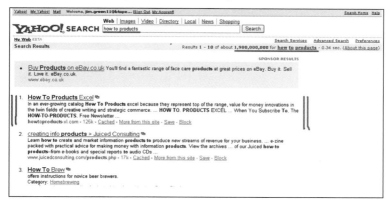

TIP

Always use your own counsel in the final selection of power keywords. You know your own concept inside out (or at least, you should) so if you have an instinctive feeling about a certain key phrase of your own choosing and it doesn't come out top on profitability – retain it nevertheless. Hunches frequently pay off handsomely in power keyword selection.

HOW KEYWORD POWER IMPACTS ON SALES

Because keyword power is the catalyst that directs visitors to your website, it follows that attention to keyword selection is crucial if you are to attract sales for the end product of your business idea. When people find you and your niche idea on the search engines they are invariably looking for something for nothing and if you provide them with freebies in the form of useful articles, tools, tips and techniques (but not too much or you'll give the store away) they will be all the more amenable to purchasing your product or service.

They won't all rush to buy, so if sales are slow to begin with, take heart, you are on track with your niche idea. Persist and the flow of transactions will gradually increase.

Think about this: According to search engine statistics an average of 121,347 people are searching on the internet every day for 'business to business' information.

Think, too, about this …

Many of these same people will be among your visitors who will find you because they want to do what they think you do: *operate a business to business service*. Okay, so you don't, so what? Many of them will still be prospects for your specific proposition.

In the light of this, it is sound practice to include two or more keywords aimed at these highly-targeted prospects. They will be seeking free information, so give them what they want for free and a percentage of them will give you a sale for your small business niche product or service.

FREE SOFTWARE TO ASSIST YOU IN DETECTING POWER KEYWORDS

Here is the tool I use in my own searches for powerful niche keywords and it comes complete with easy-to-understand instructions. Basically, what you do is feed in a niche keyword and the software will not only tell you how many people have searched for the term during the previous four weeks but also provide a detailed list of similar keywords and a precise indication of their popularity.

You may download this tool free of charge at **Good keywords**: www.goodkeywords.com.

15
How to avoid search engine positioning mistakes

Having covered the vital significance of keyword selection, and before revealing in the next chapter a failsafe system for snaring the robotic spiders, let us now turn our attention to a series of deadly errors internet marketers consistently commit when getting their websites ready for search engine submission. Don't fall into this trap when preparing your own mini- or maxi-site. Here's a list of the 10 most common mistakes. By avoiding them you will also be avoiding a lot of anguish and frustration in the long run.

OPTIMISING THE WEBSITE FOR INAPPROPRIATE KEYWORDS

The first step in any search engine optimisation campaign is to choose the keywords. We have already covered how to research and locate these, but we'll deal now with other vital considerations in relation to search engine implementation. If you initially choose the wrong keywords, all the time and effort that you devote in trying to get your site a high ranking will go down the drain. If you choose keywords which no one searches for or if you choose keywords which won't bring in targeted traffic to your site, what good will the top rankings do for your venture?

OVERLOADING THE META TAG WITH KEYWORDS

I often see sites which have hundreds of keywords listed in the Meta

Keywords tag in the hope that by listing the keywords in the Meta Keywords tag they will be able to get a high ranking for those keywords. Nothing could be further from the truth. Contrary to popular opinion, the Meta Keywords tag has almost completely lost its importance as far as search engine positioning is concerned. Hence, just by listing keywords in the Meta Keywords tag, you will never be able to get a high ranking. To get a high ranking for those keywords, you need to position them in the actual body content of your site, following the format detailed in Chapter 12.

REPLICATING THE SAME KEYWORDS OVER AND OVER AGAIN

Another common mistake is endlessly to repeat target keywords in the body of pages and in the Meta Keywords tags. Because so many people have used this tactic in the past (and continue to use it), the search engines keep a sharp lookout, and may penalise a site which repeats keywords in this fashion. Sure, you do need to repeat the keywords a number of times. But, the way you place them in your pages must make grammatical sense. Simply repeating keywords endlessly is an exercise that no longer works. Furthermore, a particular keyword should ideally not be present more than three times in your Meta Keywords tag and your text.

USING THE HIDDEN TEXT TECHNIQUE

Hidden text is text with the same colour as the background colour of your page. For example, if the background colour of your page is white and you have added some white text to that page that is considered as hidden text.

This is how it works – or rather *does not* work in practice.

Many webmasters, in order to get high rankings in the search engines, try to make their pages as keyword rich as possible. However, there is a limit to the number of keywords you can repeat in a page without making it sound odd to your human visitors as they read the copy. Thus, in order to guarantee that visitors to a page don't perceive the text to be peculiar (but at the same time maintaining keyword-rich content), some webmasters add text containing keywords in the same colour as the background colour. This ensures that while the search engines can see the keywords, the human visitors cannot. The search engines have long since caught up with this technique, and ignore or penalise the pages which contain such text. They may also penalise the *entire site* if even one of the pages in that site contains such hidden text. Don't use the hidden text technique; it's not worth it …

CREATING PAGES WITH AN OVER-ABUNDANCE OF GRAPHICS AND MARGINAL TEXT

The search engines only understand text – they don't understand graphics. Hence, if your site contains lots of graphics but little text, it is unlikely to get a high ranking in the search engines. To improve your rankings, you need to replace the graphics by keyword-rich text for the search engine spiders to feed on.

INCORPORATING KEYWORD-RICH TEXT IN THE 'NO FRAMES' TAG

Many search engines don't understand 'frames'. For sites which have used frames, these search engines only consider what is present in the NOFRAMES tag. Yet, many webmasters make the mistake of adding something like this to the NOFRAMES tag: 'This site uses frames but your browser doesn't support them'. For the search engines which don't understand frames, this is all the text that they ever get to see in this site, which means that the chances of this site getting a good ranking in these search engines are non-existent. Hence, if your site uses frames, you need to add a lot of keyword rich text to the NOFRAMES tag.

USING PAGE CLOAKING

Page cloaking is a technique used to deliver different web pages under different circumstances. People generally use page cloaking for two reasons:

1. To hide the source code of their search-engine optimised pages from their competitors and ...

2. To prevent human visitors from having to see a page which looks good to the search engines but does not necessarily look good to them.

The problem with this is that when sites use the cloaking technique it prevents the search engines from being able to spider the same page that their users are going to see. And if the search engines can't do this they can no longer be confident of providing relevant results to their users. Thus, if a search engine discovers that a site has used cloaking it will probably ban the site forever from their index. Hence, my advice is that you should not even think about using cloaking in your site.

OVER-RELIANCE ON AUTOMATIC SUBMISSION TOOLS

In order to save time many people use run-of-the-mill automatic submission software or a service to submit their sites to the major search engines. It is true that submitting your site manually to the search engines takes a lot of time and that an automatic submission tool can help you save a lot of time. However, the search engines don't like these tools and may ignore your pages if you use them. In my opinion the major search engines are simply too important for you not to spend the time to submit your site manually – that is if you decide not to do what I'm suggesting next ...

There is a legitimate way to avoid this tiresome process. When you host your website with either Third Sphere or Site Build It! they do it all for you at no extra cost. What's more to the point, the automatic software they use is state-of-the-art and perfectly acceptable to the major search engines.

OVER-SUBMITTING PAGES ON A DAILY BASIS

People often make the mistake of submitting too many pages per day to the search engines. This often results in the search engines simply ignoring many of the pages which have been submitted from that site. Ideally, you should submit no more than one page per day to the search engines. While many search engines accept more than one page per day from a particular domain there are some majors which do not. Hence, by limiting yourself to a maximum of one page per day you ensure that you stay within the limits of all the search engines.

OVER-CONCENTRATION ON SEARCH ENGINE SUBMISSION

Here's the final common mistake that people make when it comes to search engine optimisation – they spend too much time over it when they opt to do it manually. Sure, search engine placement is the most cost effective way of driving traffic to your site and you do need to spend some time every day learning how the search engines work in optimising your site. However, you must remember that search engine optimisation is a means to an end for you – it's not the end in itself. The end is to increase the sales of your products and services. Hence, apart from trying to improve your site's position in the search engines, you also need to spend time on all the other factors which determine the success or the failure of your website – the quality of the products and services that you are selling, the quality of your customer service, and so on. You may have excellent rankings in the search engines but if the quality of your produce is poor, or if your customer service leaves a lot to be desired, those high rankings aren't going to do much good.

TIP

I appreciate that the foregoing comes across as a great deal extra to take on board while shackled with the time-consuming offline tasks in the development of your small business. But look at it this way: even if you decide to do it all automatically using one of my preferred hosting options you still need to understand the basics if you are to appreciate the results. I do. Why not you?

16
Snaring the spiders to generate top ten rankings on demand

Whether your objective is to create and maintain a local or a global online presence for your small business, the work you will do to hit the target is the same, and it can prove very tiresome unless you know what you are doing and, more importantly, exactly why you are doing it. The spiders are the electronic robots dispatched by all search engines to assess your website for keywords, content and links value; the stuff that determines where, if at all, your site will be positioned in the listings. Chapters 12, 14 and 15 cover these elements in detail and my purpose here is to provide you with assistance you won't find anywhere else to ensure that your website is always positioned in the top ten rankings.

And so, rather than delve into the well-catalogued and mind boggling intricacies of search engine optimisation, I am going to disclose the simple fail-safe technique I devised and always use for *ultra-optimisation*; a technique which you too are at liberty to employ from now on.

IT WORKS FOR ME AND IT WILL WORK FOR YOU

Let me give you a recent example of its power before I give you the technique …

Within 72 hours of submission to the search engines the temporary web page for one of my projects:

http://howtobecomefamousonline.howtoproducts-xl.com

captured the No.1 Spot on Yahoo!, AltaVista, All The Web and MSN.

My exclusive technique also generated Top 10 Rankings for all of the following websites; marketing produce which I created myself.

http://howtoproducts-xl.com

http://howtoproducts-xl.com/madhatter.html

http://howtoproducts-xl.com/2.html

http://howtoproducts-xl.com/ccc.html

http://howtoproducts-xl.com/niche.html

http://costcutters.howtoproducts-xl.com

http://makingmoneyonline-xl.com

http://1st-creative-writing-course.com

http://1st-creative-writing-course.com/makemoney.html

http://1st-creative-writing-course.com/gettingpublished.html

http://1st-creative-writing-course.com/wfp.html

http://1st-creative-writing-course.com/makemoney.html

http://1st-creative-writing-course.com/starting/starting.html

http://1st-creative-writing-course.com/homeshopoffice/online.html

http://1st-creative-writing-course.com/mistakes/acm.html

http://1st-creative-writing-course.com/progress/pro.html

http://start-a-business-masterplan.com

http://retirement-moneymakers.com

http://free-stuff-xl.com

THE TECHNIQUE – YOURS TO COPY – YOURS TO KEEP

Use this 6-point core keyword phrase strategy to seduce the search engine spiders into loving your website.

1. Use your core keyword phrase as your domain name.

2. Use your core keyword phrase as your index page heading.

3. Use your core keyword phrase as your site title tag.

4. Use your core keyword phrase as your site description tag.

5. Use your core keyword phrase to start the keywords tag.

6. Use your core keyword phrase as the linchpin in your web page copy.

HOW IT WORKS IN PRACTICE

I can best demonstrate this remarkably efficient strategy by breaking down the elements as they apply to the website that grabbed three No.1 Spots within 72 hours of submitting the URL.

http://howtobecomefamousonline.howtoproducts-xl.com

1. Domain name

You see how the core keyword phrase is also domain name – or to be more precise: sub-domain in this instance.

Keyword phrase

'how to become famous online'

URL

http://howtobecomefamousonline.howtoproducts-xl.com

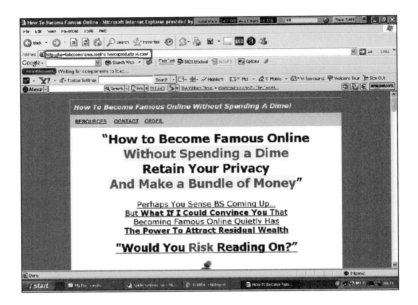

2. Index page heading

The first line of the index (home) page heading is also the core keyword phrase …

'How to Become Famous Online
Without Spending a Dime
Retain Your Privacy
And Make a Bundle of Money'

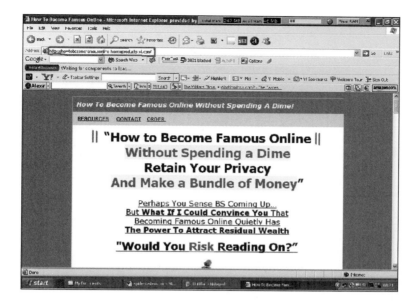

3. Site title tag

It reads <How To Become Famous Online>.

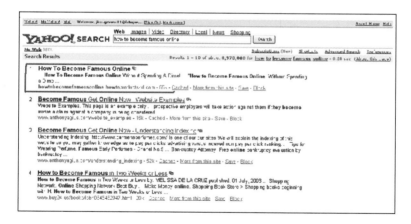

Check this out for yourself by visiting the website, right clicking, and then clicking again on 'View Source'.

4. Site description tag

It reads <How to become famous online without spending a dime, retain your privacy, and make a bundle of money>.

Note how the entire headline of the index page constitutes the Meta tag description.

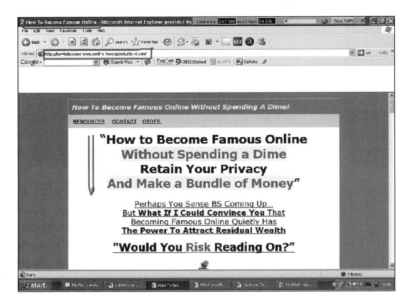

Again, check this out for yourself by visiting the website, right clicking, and then clicking again on 'View Source'.

5. Keyword tag

It reads < how to, become famous, online, income streams, residual, search engines>.

Note how I have broken down the words in the title tag into three separate keyword phrases: how to, become famous, online which combine to start the keywords tag ...

Yet again, check this out for yourself by visiting the website, right clicking and then clicking again on 'View Source'.

See how DOMAIN NAME + TITLE TAG + KEYWORDS TAG + SITE DESCRIPTION TAG link together to snare the spiders.

6. Keyword phrase as the linchpin in your copy

Visit the web page and see how I have interlaced the copy with the keywords; majoring on the keyword phrase and peppering up the text with the other keywords.

The secret lies in strategic positioning; always include keywords and keyword phrases judiciously.

See how my copy flows; flows so naturally that you are completely unaware that it is peppered with those vital core phrases.

FOLLOW THIS TRIED AND TESTED TECHNIQUE AND YOU WILL HIT THE HIGH SPOTS

You will get top ten positions for your core keywords, *but only* after you have mastered all of the strategies in this book. This is essential because to have the system work perfectly, everything must be in position so that you can view the mix as a whole and fuse its various elements to produce the desired results. When you have achieved that you will be in a position to fast forward the entire system by downloading the master version. It contains 70 dynamic pages of instruction and costs $47 (approx. £26.34), is worth at least ten times the price – but you as a reader of this book, can get it for free. Send a blank email to jimgreen@writing-for-profit.com with '*Spiders*' in the subject line and I'll get back to you with the download link. You don't absolutely *need* the master but if you have ownership it will certainly speed up your capacity for generating top ten spots for your core keywords.

And now if you'd like a little more detail on basic search engine optimisation, I can offer you this article from an online friend ...

OVERCOMING SEARCH ENGINE PARALYSIS

Many do-it-yourself webmasters and online entrepreneurs have been led to believe that search engine positioning is a black art and that no mere amateur can hope to compete with the 'experts.' If you are among them, you're missing out on a great opportunity to drive free, targeted traffic to your website.

There are only three steps you need to take, if you want to quickly increase your site's visibility in the search engines. The three steps are: positioning, optimisation, and link building. In this short tutorial, I'll explain what's involved in each one, and show you just how easy it can be. If you can give me even 10 minutes of your time today, you'll be well on your way to top rankings.

If there is one message I'd like to get across to you, it's 'don't fear the search engines.' Not everything that you have been told about them is true! If you would like to increase the amount of traffic flowing to your website, without spending a dime, I urge you to read this article with an open mind.

Step 1: Keyword Research & Search Term Selection

Let's start with a quick definition: *Search terms* are the words and phrases that people type into search engines. For example, if I go to Google.com and type in 'pokemon cards'; that's a search term.

To get traffic from search engines you need to know what people are searching for and who you're competing against. This sounds very basic but it's important. Search term selection really boils down to finding a balance between popularity, targeting, and competition.

Realtors, for example, might be tempted when they discover how many people search for 'real estate,' and believe that this is a perfect set of keywords. That's a very popular search term, but unless you sell real estate all over the world, it's not specific enough to reach your customers.

Some folks can come up with good, targeted search terms with nothing more than common sense, but I prefer to do my homework. The best way to do this on your own is with the Wordtracker service www.wordtracker.com which allows you to find popular search terms, and investigate the competition.

If you aren't interested in doing it yourself, you can hire someone to do the research for you, and get a report back that tells you which search terms are the most popular, and which will be the easiest to compete for.

Low-cost keyword research reports are available from SEO Research Labs www.seoresearchlabs.com and you can find any number of competing services by looking up 'keyword research' on your favorite search engine.

Step 2: Search Engine Optimisation

Optimising simply means putting the keywords you've selected onto your web pages in the right places with the right formatting. That's all it means. There's a great deal of misinformation about this subject, so let me set the record straight: optimising is the easiest part of this process.

How easy is it? Well, I can tell you 90 per cent of what you need to know in just a few lines and there's a good chance that you'll never need to learn the rest. Once you see what you can accomplish though, you'll probably want to learn more.

The first thing to understand is that you should only use 1-2 search terms to optimise each page. Once you've selected a page to optimise and the search terms you're going to use, all you have to do is put those words in the right places and you're done.

Where the search terms go:

1. Your page's TITLE tag;

2. Your 'keywords' and 'description' META tags;

3. In a heading tag (H1, H2, or H3) near the top of the page;

4. In the first paragraph of body text, and repeated 1-2 more times on the page;

5. In the text of any links that point to the page;

That's 90 per cent of search engine optimisation right there. The most important of these are no. 1, no. 3, and no. 4. Just try it, it works. My *Inside Out Marketing* site uses no META tags at all, and it gets traffic for hundreds of search terms every month.

Step 3: Link Building & Link Popularity

Link building simply means getting other websites to link to yours. If you aren't already working on this, you need to start. Even if you don't care about search engines, those links will bring in traffic on their own and help you establish a credible reputation for your website.

Link building is an important part of search engine positioning because search engines look at these links as a 'vote' for your website, and they will boost your rankings accordingly when other sites link to you.

There are three simple ways to improve your site's link popularity and drive traffic at the same time:

a) *Submit your site to the major directories*. Yahoo charges $299 a year for commercial sites, but there are several popular directories, including dmoz.org, goguides.org, and joeant.com, that will list your site for free.

b) *Trade links with related websites*. You can help each other, and your visitors, by linking to other good websites.

c) *Look for other sites that have resource directories*, and ask them to link to you. I like to look in the Open Directory www.dmoz.org to find related sites.

Whatever you do, don't try to take 'shortcuts' when it comes to building links. If you'd like to learn more about link building, try Linking 101 http://www.linking101.com and Linking Matters http://www.linkingmatters.com.

That's it! If you do these three simple things your search engine rankings are sure to improve. Just remember that there are no shortcuts, and it's never a good idea to try to trick the search engines.

The honest approach is easier and much better for you and your visitors'.

About the Author

Dan Thies is the author of *Search Engine Fast Start!* a concise guide to positioning your site with the new breed of search engines. Visit www.cannedbooks.com

FOOTNOTE

To round off matters on capturing the top spots using my system I'd like to introduce you to an exceptional free tool that will allow you to keep daily tabs on your rankings and keyword effectiveness. You will find it at http://mikes-marketing-tools.com

17
Creating site maps to feed the spiders

Google were first to introduce site maps and then Yahoo! quickly followed suit. So far I have only used them for one of my websites www.writing-for-profit.com and I have to say it has helped maintain my No.1 spot out of 44,900,000 competitive web pages at Google. With the hullabaloo going on right now about the significance of site maps I would be doing you less than justice not to mention them and I can do no better than reproduce this informative article on the subject with the compliments of the author ...

Your site map: spider food or just a light snack?

Karon Thackston © 2005

'Mechanical spiders have to eat. In fact they usually have bigger appetites than the real-life spiders you squish under your shoe. It's hard work roaming around the internet non-stop and these little chaps need some nourishment from time-to-time. In fact, when spiders find some hearty spider food (a.k.a. a site map with some meat to it) they sit down to stay a while – and that's a good thing.

You may have seen some site maps. The standard ones look like the example on the next page with each phrase being linked to the page of the same (or similar) name.

Site maps are deemed spider food because they can be the perfect place for search engine spiders and bots to crawl your site and, because a site map has links to every page of your site (and those link names or page descriptions often include keywords), it is extremely easy for the search engine spider to access each publicly accessible

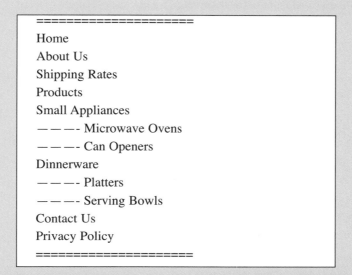

```
=====================
Home
About Us
Shipping Rates
Products
Small Appliances
— — —- Microwave Ovens
— — —- Can Openers
Dinnerware
— — —- Platters
— — —- Serving Bowls
Contact Us
Privacy Policy
=====================
```

area with no obstacles and relate it to a given subject matter. (For example, a page labeled 'microwave ovens' is most likely about microwave ovens.)

Some site owners think that's enough. They think a page with keyword-rich titles and links is plenty for a hungry little spider to munch on. Hardly; that's not a meal, it's just a light snack.

Give spiders a tasty treat

If you really want to fill the spiders' bellies, you'll want to take your site map page to the max with a descriptive site map (as I like to call them). Descriptive site maps go beyond the simple list of links to pages. These special versions of the traditional maps also include a short, keyword-rich description of each page. The text only needs to be a sentence or two in length but get creative and use columns, bullets or other formatting to make it look the way you like. (The links would remain the same as in the previous example.)

Descriptive site maps work well in attracting and satisfying spiders because they include naturally occurring keywords. They also place keywords in the vicinity of a link that points to the associated page.

Add these advantages to those that already exist, including:

- Having links in the body copy of the page;
- Overcoming complex navigation such as DHTML or Java;
- Lending quick access to pages located several layers deep within the site;
- Assisting with usability for visitors (especially disabled visitors).

Do it this way and you will have prepared a huge feast for the search engine spiders that is almost guaranteed to entice those hungry little creatures to crawl through every available page of your site.

Does every site need a site map?

It certainly wouldn't hurt. Sites with fewer than 20 pages or sites where most or all the pages have links directly from the home page generally don't need a site map, per se. However, practically every site of every size can reap benefits from the inclusion of one.

If you're creating a site map for your site, don't stop with the basics. With just a little added effort, you'll have a four-course meal to serve the spiders that will keep them happy and satisfied and that will help get you exceptional rankings.'

Karon Thackston

www.copywritingcourse.com/keyword

18

Flooding your site with low- and no-cost traffic

The bulk of the traffic to your website will come from the major search engines, but there are several other low- and no-cost avenues to explore and, if used correctly and regularly, they can flood your site with traffic.

INVESTING IN THE PAY-PER-CLICK SEARCH ENGINES

Search engine optimisation is a skilled exercise with no guarantee of sustained success for even the most competitive keywords. Equally, paid submissions cannot guarantee top positions for your web pages; they can only guarantee indexing in the search engine database. You may still come up in the hundredth page of search results.

These factors have made pay-per-click (PPC) search engines an important element of any website promotion campaign. Actually, these engines could also be called pay-for-position search engines. You could bid for the number one position in search results for the keyword you choose. If there are many bidders you would have to bid high (in pounds instead of pence for every single visitor to secure a top position). You then pay at the bid rate for every click-through to your website; hence, pay-per-click.

The best strategy for the PPC element of your campaign is to bid for a number of less competitive keywords that are important to you. This could be significantly less expensive than bidding for one high competition keyword. Finding bid prices for the keywords, submitting bids for all these, and then tracking the results for each is a tedious exercise. However, there are tools to automate much of this tiresome work and with one of these you could focus on selecting the keywords to bid for and leave the rest to the tool.

PARTICIPATING IN NEWSGROUPS, FORUMS, MAILING LISTS

The second tactic is to participate in targeted forums and newsgroups. It's free. You start visiting the forum regularly and then once you know your way around it you should start answering questions for people and becoming an all-round helpful individual. Give and it will be given back to you.

You will be able to build up relationships in these forums and build up your traffic at the same time without ever having to spend a penny. To find out more about how to participate in forums for maximum traffic, check out this free report:

www.bizpromo.com/free/networking.htm

The best places to find the actual forums and newsgroups are:

- Forums can be found at www.forumone.com;
- Newsgroups can be searched at http://groups.google.com/;
- Mailing Lists are found at www.liszt.com.

EXCHANGING LINKS WITH OTHER WEBSITES

Another no-cost marketing technique is to trade links with other websites. Now, I know from experience this can be a daunting task at first ... you trade 10 links and only get an ounce of traffic from it ... but what happens when you start having hundreds or thousands of *related sites* linked to you? You get a flood of visitors, that's what.

Where do you start? Start by getting out there and offering: offer to trade links with people who are in the same forums, newsgroups, and mailing lists as you. Go to some of the online databases that have links. Participate in banner exchanges and link exchanges. Nothing will happen unless you take the initiative and do something.

For top resources in this area, check out:

www.whitepalm.com/fourcorners/linkswapping.shtml

www.netofficetoolbox.com

We'll be covering the power of linking in greater detail in Chapter 21.

CREATING ARTICLES FOR NEWSLETTERS AND MAGAZINES

There are thousands of newsletters and magazines out there just waiting for your articles. What is your area of expertise? Write about it or, if you don't want to do the writing yourself, collect the information together in an organised manner and have someone else do it for you. Once you have your highly informative article ready to go, contact publishers of ezines and magazines and submit your piece. Think about the publicity you can get through this. It can bring thousands of people to your site with almost no cost at all.

For information on ezines, check out:

www.netofficetoolbox.com/

For the Top Media Directory for Offline Publications, go to:

www.gebbieinc.com

In Chapter 20 I'll let you in on my own secrets on how to milk this no-cost method to attract thousands of targeted visitors to your website.

USING CGI TRAFFIC PLUG-INS ON YOUR WEBSITE

There are many CGI programs out there which can help become traffic generators by having your visitors return over and over again. Tools such as classified ad sites, free-for-all link pages, message boards, chat rooms, postcard sites, and more can all contribute to your overall traffic-building plan. Many of these programs can be added to your website for little or no money. Take a look at this resource for finding these types of scripts:

www.cgi-resources.com/Programs_and_Scripts/Perl

For many people, though, installing a CGI program may be the nightmare. For those of you who are technically challenged, CGI Resource has a list of places where you can have your traffic plug-ins remotely hosted for you. Check out their remotely hosted scripts at:

www.cgi-resources.com

TRIGGERING INTEREST WITH FREE PRESS RELEASES

Don't just think it takes knowing the right people to get your press releases out. It doesn't. If you can give the media stories which are interesting and revealing, they will be glad to publish them.

- Do you have a new exciting product?

- Do you have an event going on at your site that's newsworthy?

Come up with one and then contact the media.

Here are two services I use where you can do it all for free:

www.prweb.com
www.free-press-release.com

When someone asks you to plunk down money for an ad (as they will), check back on these six ways to advertise your site for little or no cost. Many of them can create awesome traffic at your site and don't cost a penny. The ones which do have a small cost to them can produce traffic worth far more than many of the ads out there.

To promote an internet website does not require a large advertising budget. Those who have a large budget at their disposal also labour under a big disadvantage when marketing online; they pay for ad after ad and end up losing most of their money. Online, the best things in life are free.

19
Converting your expertise into digital produce

Now you are about to discover just how easy it is to convert your expertise into the first digitised produce for your small enterprise, how to package it, how to market it – but before we start – check that you have attended to the following:

- You've got it all down on paper;

- You've explained what your product, your service, your solution is all about;

- You've listed the features;

- You've highlighted the benefits;

- You've established what you don't know;

- You've rectified the information shortfall by researching;

- You've researched until you've located all you still needed to learn;

- You've identified your market;

- You've discovered how to reach it;

- You've learned how to test market;

- You've committed to learning how to promote.

If you are in any doubt about any item on this list go back to Chapter 4 for refreshment and then come back here ...

HOW TO CREATE YOUR OWN DIGITAL INFORMATION PRODUCE

It's as easy as pie. Once you are completely satisfied with the text for your project you simply pop it into the software compiler of your choice and out comes the finished information product. You can include graphics, illustrations, pictures, flow charts, etc. – whatever, in fact, you reckon will add glitz to the overall effect.

CHOICE OF FORMATTING SYSTEMS

For formatting you have a choice of …

EXE (short for Executable Extension and pronounced *ee-ex-ee*) – an executable file with an .exe extension.

PDF (short for Portable Document Format) – a file format developed by Adobe Systems. PDF captures formatting information from a variety of desktop publishing applications, making it possible to send formatted documents and have them appear on the recipient's monitor or printer as they were intended. To view a file in PDF format, you need Adobe Reader, a free application distributed by Adobe Systems.

EXE produces complete documents in minutes whereas PDF does the same job in seconds. Of the two, my personal preference is PDF and not just because it's faster; it provides a more polished finish, it can be read on any computer screen anywhere in the world – and it's cheaper- sometimes completely free.

COMPILER FOR EXE PRODUCTION

www.ebookgenerator.com

COMPILER OPTIONS FOR PDF PRODUCTION

Be careful shopping around for PDF compilers. You can get ripped off mercilessly by fly-by-night shysters telling you how difficult the system is to master and trying to sell you expensive instruction courses. It's not at all difficult; it is simplicity itself.

Here are the compilers I use for my information produce. They are excellent and for both you are allowed to create your first ebooks for free.

Adobe PDF Online – free trial/5 ebooks/100MB capacity for each book. Access it at www.adobe.com.

deskPDF – same deal but thereafter $19.95 (approx. £11) for permanent usage. Find it at www.docudesk.com.

Explore the alternative systems for compilation and decide for yourself with which you feel the most comfortable.

HOW TO CREATE VIRTUAL BOOK COVERS AUTOMATICALLY

When your first ebook rolls off the assembly line you will want to wrap it in a professionally produced cover and, until recently, design and creation would have set you back between £75 and £125 per cover. Not any more. There are now several software tools available that do it all for you.

WHY IT IS IMPORTANT TO HAVE A COVER FOR YOUR INFORMATION PRODUCT

It's very important, and here's why. When people browse around bookstores the first thing to capture their attention is the cover. That's stage one in the decision-making process: to buy or not to buy. The same thing applies with online browsers on the lookout for virtual books to purchase, and you will greatly enhance your chances of success if all your e-produce is appropriately packed. After all, who buys a book, offline or online, without an opportunity of glancing at the cover to discover what's inside?

Here are two examples of the best in ebook cover generation software.

ebook Cover Generator – Costs $97 (approx. £53) to purchase outright. No free trial. See www.ebookcovergenerator.com.

Virtual Cover Creator – Costs $67 (approx. £37) but offers an unlimited free trial to enable you to become familiar with complete software. You won't be able to use the end produce in the trial version because it will be watermarked until you part with the cash to purchase. Find it at www.virtualcovercreator.com.

My personal preference is for the latter option which I use for all my e-produce.

CREATING YOUR STRATEGY FOR SALES AND DISTRIBUTION

We covered the bones of this in Chapter 4 but you will be provided in Chapter 26 with a detailed strategy for automatic order-taking and product fulfilment. Suffice to say here that when you have everything else in position, sales and distribution form the simplest aspect of the exercise.

WHY IT WILL PAY YOU TO GIVE SOME OF YOUR EBOOKS AWAY FOR FREE

Believe it or not, you will sell more information products online if you start by giving some away for free. Here is how it works. You have created your first ebook, set the price, automated order-taking and distribution, and are raring to go. What you do now is to produce a mini 'taster' version to give away free of charge to your website visitors. You should start the taster with a 'flat' book cover (don't worry, the software shows you how to do this), followed by your preface or introduction, one or two sample chapters, and culminating in your entire sales page complete with ordering instructions. Most people will pick up anything for free online and you will be amazed how many are persuaded to purchase directly from the taster. You are dealing with targeted prospects and giving them two bites at the cherry. It's like allowing them to turn the pages as they would in a physical bookstore.

Have a look at how I do it when you call at my website to collect the free information produce I'll be offering you at the end of this chapter.

Better still: proceed then to visit my main website http://howtoproducts-xl.com where you can view a panorama of e-covers for my personally generated produce.

HOW TO CREATE YOUR OWN SOFTWARE PROGRAMS

Even if you don't know how to write a single line of code you can create your own exclusive software programs in 30 minutes – or your money back according to the vendors. This startling new invention (patent pending) creates an infinite number of high-demand software programs which you can sell royalty-free at any price.

You can access complete details of the amazing new tool that is currently sweeping the web by visiting this website: www.MakeYourOwnSoftware.com/bestsellers.

TIP

I recently purchased an excellent tome on the subject of digitising information produce. 'Simple Guide to Creating Ebooks' is the title and it cost me $49.95 – but you, as a valued reader, can have it for free. Here is what to do: Visit my website www.writing-for-profit.com. Click on the button marked 'FREE eBOOK' in the navigation bar, fill in a simple form, and the download links for your free copy plus 2 bonus books will be emailed straight back to you. Enjoy ...

20
Using the amazing authority of zero cost articles to lure visitors

Engaging in online marketing without access to the strategies revealed in this book is akin to entering a giant 'mugs alley' in a virtual fairground where all the vendors are barking out their sales pitches to each other because there's no one else around to listen in. You won't have that problem. What you are absorbing here is a series of tried and tested techniques of enticing visitors onto your stall to listen to your message to the exclusion of competing distractions.

Now here's another such technique and a vital one at that ...

WHY ALL SUCCESSFUL E-ENTREPRENEURS USE ARTICLES TO ATTRACT VISITORS

They cost nothing but time and energy to produce and distribute, and the power they exert is astounding.

Article submission is the perfect niche vehicle for attracting pre-qualified, targeted prospects for your niche produce at zero cost.

- You should adopt this influential practice for your own online promotion;
- You will miss out on a potential gold mine of buyers if you do not.

You know all there is to know about your first online project; you even produced an information product on the topic.

Now is the time to make a start on your first batch of articles.

HOW TO MAKE A START

Pull down strands of useful information from your information product; sculpt it into a dozen or so initial articles for distribution (I'll show you how, why and where in a moment).

When you think you've exhausted that source, go back to your research notes and you will find more; much more.

When you've finished doing that, go back online and research again. Look at what other people have to say about the topic, not to copy them, but to use whatever you glean to prompt you to search in disparate directions.

Then do likewise at discussion forums. The supply of information is endless.

WRITING YOUR FIRST ARTICLE FOR GENERAL DISTRIBUTION

You will get the hang of it very quickly and when you do, you will be churning out one or two articles at a time, quite effortlessly. There are just a few simple rules to observe.

1. Start with an eye-grabbing headline.
2. Fire your biggest gun in the first sentence.
3. Fire the next biggest in the next sentence or two.
4. Keep the text rolling on with short chunky paragraphs.
5. Break it up with occasional subheadings.
6. Keep it conversational.
7. Restrict the word count to between 500 and 700.
8. End with a resource box (your bio).

Here now is a text example of one of my own articles which is shown again in published format immediately after …

Fact: Start a Business Without A Masterplan For Success And You Are 95% Certain to Fail!

Fact: Only 5% of People Who Start a Business Make it into Year 6.

95% of small business start-ups fail within 5 years. Two-thirds of new employer firms survive at least two years, and about half survive at least four years.

(Source: Small Business Administration 2004).

How can this be when the same US Government source claims that small firms represent more than 99.7% of all employers? Why is the failure rate so high? Here's why. 95% of all start-ups have no masterplan in position at the outset and in consequence flounder and sink without a trace. What's more, this alarming fatality quotient applies equally to offline and online enterprises. Even worse, tens of thousands more start a business every day and follow exactly the same route to disaster.

Fact: Google lists in excess of 12,000,000 websites offering advice on how to start a business – but how many I wonder emanate from people who've actually done it for themselves? My site does. I've founded, owned and operated dozens of small businesses – and I'm still doing it. I've also authored two widely-acclaimed best-selling hard copy books on the topic, 'Starting Your Own Business' (How To Books ISBN 1-85703-859-2) and 'Starting an Internet Business at Home' (Kogan Page ISBN 0-7494-3484-8); titles that sell in big numbers online at Amazon.com and offline in bookstores throughout the world.

Now I'm unzipping my case notes spanning 40 years of successful independent commercial activity to present you with an all-in-one masterplan to ensure success before you start a business – and to maintain momentum in tandem with your endeavors so that you don't end up in the same place as 95% of start-ups: the dump truck.

The All-in-One Start a Business Masterplan doesn't simply focus on getting you up and running. As the Ultimate Start a Business Compendium it goes deeper, much deeper. In its 4 individual tutorials it aims at the creative heart of operating a small enterprise: how to start a business with failsafe offline and online strategies, how to avoid the crucial mistakes that cripple 95% of all start-ups, and how to sustain progress with tried, tested, proven stratagems.

Blueprint for fulfilment before you start a business

The All-in-One Start a Business Masterplan will empower you to conceive your own exclusive blueprint for a happy, successful and rewarding small business operation. Plans are great things. They show you where you are going, what to do, and how to do it when you get there. Make no mistake though; you will not be creating this blueprint just to get you started. It's going to be around for a long time and you will want to review and update it regularly to take account of twists and turns along the way. That's the beauty of it. When you have a blueprint for success, you can legislate for change. Without one you cannot; you'll be like the explorer in the jungle without a map.

The All-In-One Start a Business Master Plan

What this is not is a hotchpotch of miscellaneous lame-brained notions and opinions cobbled together to create a sycophantic litany. The All-in-One Start a Business Masterplan is the genuine product of my own personal experience as a successful small business owner offline and online.

It consists of 4 comprehensive tutorials, 60 full blown chapters, 555 pages, and covers every aspect of single-minded entrepreneurship: galvanizing into initial action, getting started on your plan, settling on an idea for your enterprise, tackling initial teething problems, overcoming the threatening scenarios everyone encounters along the way, and setting the course for a lifetime of fulfilment and enrichment.

The good, the bad, and the in-between are all recorded: where I hit the target plumb center, where I screwed up, and how I put it right.

Jim Green is a successful Networker and bestselling author with a string of niche non-fiction titles to his credit. His All-In-One Tutorial is available at www.writing-for-profit.com/start-a-business.html

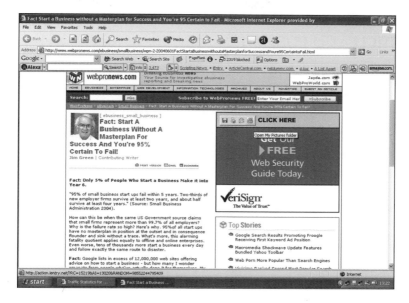

This article appeared in Web Pro News (the leading online magazine) and attracted 2,071 additional visitors to my website in just 14 days

Does promoting with articles always work to drive huge numbers of visitors to your site instantly every single time you do it?

No.

The truth is not every single article you write and distribute online will hit a home run and bring an avalanche of visitors to your site.

Some of my articles only attract a trickle, but I have so many of them out there now that in total they add up to a sizeable volume of steady, targeted traffic.

Periodically I hit a grand slam with an article that takes on a life of its own and dumps thousands of visitors on my site in a couple of days – like the one you just read ...

THE WORST THING THAT CAN HAPPEN WITH EVERY ARTICLE YOU PUBLISH

- You continue to **build** your reputation and credibility with your target audience as a trusted expert.

- As your **credibility** increases, Joint Venture partners will begin to seek you out and be open to your approaches.

- You'll create additional tools your affiliates can use to **sell more** of your products.

- You create more **valuable content** for your own and other people's websites that the search engines can index – **driving even more traffic** to your website or affiliate link.

- You create additional instalments for your auto-responder series that you can easily turn into **profitable** mini-courses.

- You get better and better at picking topics, distributing articles and your traffic logs will **snowball with targeted visitors**.

In fact, just by writing and distributing zero cost articles on the internet, you will become recognised as a world-class expert on the topic of your choice and you will have people seeking you out for all kinds of lucrative opportunities.

Promoting with articles represents one of the best ways to not only attract free traffic but to build your business and your reputation online.

WHERE TO SUBMIT YOUR ARTICLE OUTPUT

And now to save you the time and trouble of doing it yourself, I will give you my own list of 'hubs' for article submission. You can add to this as you discover other outlets relevant to your specialist topic.

128 ARTICLE HUBS THAT DISTRIBUTE YOUR MATERIAL FOR FREE

http://ezinearticles.com

http://homeincome.com/writers-connection

http://writingcorner.com/admin/sub-guidelines.htm

theezine.net

www.abundancecenter.com

www.addme.com

www.articlebliss.com

www.article-content-king.com

www.articlecrazy.com

www.article-direct.com

www.article-directory.com

www.article-emporium.com

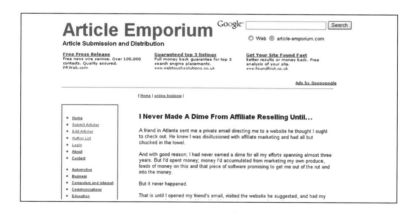

www.articlefinders.com

www.article-highway.com

www.articlehub.com

www.articlejackpot.com

www.articlelookup.com

www.articlemill.com

www.articlenexus.com

www.articlepeak.com

www.articlepoint.com

www.articlepros.com

www.articles.net

www.articles411.com

www.articles4business.com

www.articlesfactory.com

www.articleshaven.com

www.articleshelf.com

www.articleshow.com

www.articlesmagazine.com

www.articlesphere.com

www.articletime.com

www.articletogo.com

www.articlevenue.com

www.article-warehouse.com

www.articlewiz.com

www.authorconnection.com

www.bharatbhasha.com

www.bigarticles.com

www.blogtelecast.com

www.blogwidow.com

www.businessknow-how.com

www.businessknowledgesource.com

www.businessopportunity.com

www.businesstoolchest.com

www.certificate.net/wwio

www.chiff.com

www.clearviewpublications.com

www.commonconnections.com

www.content-articles.com

www.contentdesk.com

www.contentmasterworld.com

www.cumuli.com

www.digitalwomen.com

www.directarticles.com

www.ebookdeals.com

www.ebusiness-articles.com

www.e-calc.net

www.entrepreneurnewz.com

www.e-syndicate.com

www.etext.org

www.ezau.com

www.ezinecrow.com

www.ezine-writer.com.au

www.FBCmarketing.com

www.freearticlezone.com

www.freeezinesite.com

www.freelancewriting.com/newssyndicator.html

www.freesticky.com

www.fresh-articles.com

www.getyourarticles.com

www.goarticles.com

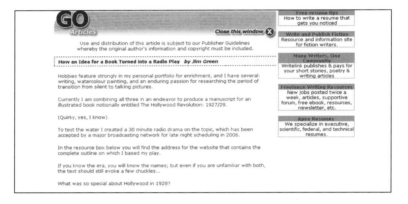

www.goodinfo.com

www.homebasedbusinessindex.com

www.home-based-business-opportunities.com/library/id2101-book.shtml

www.homebiztools.com

www.homebusinessdigest.com

www.homebusinesswebsite.com

www.homeincome.com

www.how-it-works.net

www.howtoadvice.com

www.ibizresources.com

www.ideamarketers.com

www.internetbasedmoms.com

www.jogena.com

www.learningfolder.com

www.linkgrinder.com

www.linksnoop.com

www.marketing-seek.com

www.marketingtroll.com

www.masterhomebusiness.com

www.mbnet.com

www.more4youarticledirectory.com

www.morganadvicearchive.com

www.NADmedia.com

www.netterweb.com

www.newarticlesonline.com

www.newfreearticles.com

www.onlinelists.com

www.powerhomebiz.com

www.promotiondata.com

www.purplehelp.com

www.rapidaticle.com

www.reprintarticles.com

www.searchwarp.com

www.simplysearch4it.com

www.smallbusinessportal.com

www.storebuilder.com

www.submit-your-articles.com

www.success4youmarketing.com

www.theezinedot.net

www.uncoverthenet.com

www.uniterra.com

www.upromote.com

www.vectorcentral.com

www.webmarketingspecialists.com

www.webmasterslibrary.com

www.webpromotionguru.com

www.webpronews.com

www.webreference.com

www.websitefuel.com

www.websitetrafficinfo.com

www.web-source.net/syndicator_submit.htm

www.wordpress.com

www.workoninternet.com

www.writersdigest.com

www.zinos.com

THIS SOFTWARE THAT DOES IT ALL AUTOMATICALLY

If submitting your articles manually would dig too deeply into your busy working week then consider investing in *Article Submitter*; it distributes material in bulk to all recognised sources. A new enhanced model was recently introduced and last time I looked it was still available on a free three-day-trial basis.

http://www.articlesubmitterpro.com

CONVERTING ARTICLES INTO PRESS RELEASES

We talked about press releases in Chapter 6 where I provided you with two excellent sources for distribution. While you will come across lots of advice elsewhere regarding formatting I recommend you stick with what I've just given you on construction. It works for me and it will work for you.

HOW TO DRIVE HOARDS OF TRAFFIC TO YOUR WEBSITE

Here is an extension to what you've just read that drives traffic in droves to my portal site.

Most savvy Net workers use articles on a regular basis, but I add a new dimension that produces spectacular results.

Apart from the hundreds of articles I already have circulating on the internet, I produced 20 specific 'How To' articles, each relating to a specific product.

1. Each article has its own (sub-domain); each has its own URL.

2. These pages are all posted to the Web.

3. They are all listed in the main directories, the major search engines, and in 100+ supplementary engines.

4. Included also at the foot of every web page is a link back to my portal site.

5. On the portal site there is a page entitled 'Articles' which contains individual links to each of these web pages.

On the next page is an example of one of the pages:

> ### How To Excel In The Race To Keep Pace With Online Marketing
>
> The day you stop learning about online marketing is the day to start your closing down sale.
>
> You can never learn enough let alone too much about the enigma that is online marketing.
>
> Change is ever in the air and when it strikes, it strikes like lightning, and leaves no calling card. New technologies appear overnight; old systems vanish into the ether just as quickly. Obsolescence pulls the rug out from under established multi-nationals and replaces it with it with 'blades'...
>
> Even if you're just tapping away at computer keys to turn a buck at home you must always be up to speed or you too will hit the dump truck and your online marketing activity will rapidly become little more than a hobby.
>
> So, what to do?
>
> Keep on learning.
>
> Over the years I have gathered together a catalog of 'how to' tools which have assisted me and countless others to keep pace with the ever-changing cyberspace marketplace.
>
> They comprise a mix of innovations for creative writing and strategic commerce.
>
> Why include creative writing?

All 20 web pages have a corporate look (Palatino Linotype headings and Book Antiqua for the body matter).

THIS TECHNIQUE PRODUCES STAGGERING RESULTS

These 20 pages are picking up browsers from all over the internet and driving them in droves back to my portal site. It's a case of multiple exposure, multiple viral marketing, multiple visits.

I am currently receiving more traffic from these 20 web pages than from all the major search engines combined.

Total cost: zero.

> ### TIP
>
> Whatever else you don't do in your quest to become famous online, make sure you implement the strategy I've just given you for using zero cost articles to lure visitors to your website. It is an incredibly powerful tool and one you simply cannot afford to ignore.

21
The power of linking to other websites

Another clever cost-free way of enticing the spiders and driving traffic to your website is through the power of linking to other sites; not any old sites, but sites specifically related to your topic.

Take the trouble to sniff them out by undertaking some basic research.

Try this out for size at the Google.com search engine: 'your topic + websites' and again 'your topic + articles' (replacing of course 'your topic' for **your own particular topic**).

You will be presented with a myriad of potential linking partners but you won't be linking to all of them because that would defeat the purpose: link only to those (100/500 maximum) that you sense relate most closely to your website content. Link to too many and the search engines won't be happy.

I have 423 quality links to my prime site and they consistently bring in targeted traffic that I wouldn't otherwise get.

EASY ZERO COST STEPS FOR BUILDING LINK POPULARITY

You did your homework and learned all about optimising techniques for your website. Your relevant keywords are prominently placed in all the right places on your pages. Yet your site still isn't ranking quite the way you want.

- What do you do?

- Why bother with link building?

Link popularity and link quality are very important because every major search engine now considers them as a part of their ranking algorithms.

If you don't have links, you won't rank well for competitive keywords.

If your page includes all the important on-the-page criteria and scores well with Alexa (www.alexa.com is the accepted source for measuring traffic performance of billions of web pages), it's time to focus on your links.

Good inbound links can move your page up the ranking ladder and act as new entry points to your site.

HOW DOES YOUR SITE GET THOSE COVETED INBOUND LINKS?

First off, let's make sure you understand the basics.

- **Link popularity is the measure of inbound links** to your website.

- **Link analysis evaluates which sites are linking to you** and the link text itself.

Fortunately, there are many ways to improve your link quality and popularity, which will give you a boost in the rankings. Here are some guidelines to help you set up your own linking campaign:

PREPARING YOUR SITE FIRST BEFORE YOU START LOOKING FOR LINKS

Before you start your link building campaign, take time to get your site in shape.

- Make sure your site looks professional, has good content and is easy to navigate.

- Check your links with a free tool like www.htmltoolbox.com.

If a potential 'linker' goes to your site and finds broken pages, they are not going to want to link to you.

In addition, directories have gone on record saying they may exclude sites with broken links and page errors.

Directories want only professional looking sites in their databases, so do your homework on your site before you start promoting it and your linking campaign will be more effective.

BUDGETING TIME FOR LINK BUILDING

Don't expect to grow your link popularity overnight. Budget time every week to work on link building. If you force yourself to spend a couple of hours a week on link building, it will become part of your routine.

Pick one day a week and set aside time as your link-building time. If you don't make it a priority, it won't get done. Link building is an incremental activity. Over time these one or two new links start adding up until they are into the hundreds.

ESTABLISHING REALISTIC LINKING GOALS

Don't expect to see instant results. Link building is difficult, frustrating and time intensive. Convincing another website to link to you can be exasperating. If you get one good quality link a month you're doing better than the majority of sites out there. Patience and creativity are central to link building.

- Track your progress so you know who you've asked already. It could be embarrassing to ask a site for a link if they've already given you one;

- If a website initially declines your link request, wait a while and then ask again. Their focus may change over time. A 'no' today may change into a 'yes' six to nine months later.

BE SELECTIVE ABOUT THE SITES FROM WHICH YOU REQUEST LINKS

Search engines use sophisticated rules when judging the importance of a link and the popularity of the site linking to you is a key criterion.

One link from bbc.com is worth much more than 100 links from a personal website.

And don't even think of using a 'link farm' because link farms are sites that exist solely to link to other websites. They are nothing more than a blatant attempt to inflate link popularity and search engines take a dim view of them. Google in particular has been known to ban sites found using a link farm.

Try to identify non-competitive sites in the same field as your site. Links from sites that are related to your area carry more weight than sites from Aunt Sue's fashion site. That doesn't mean you should refuse a link from Aunt Sue; just be aware it won't help you much in link quality terms. On the other hand, links from sites within the orbit of your own specialist topic are strong endorsements for your site.

DEVELOPING A RELATIONSHIP WITH A SITE

Before you ask for the link, get to know the website. Establish yourself as a real human first. That way, when you ask for a link, it's harder for them to say no. Impersonal broadcast emails asking for links are spam. Sure, it's easier, but it will only result in making another website owner mad at you. Spam link requests do not work and waste everyone's time. Don't do it.

Providing the linking code

Make it easy for other sites to link to you. Send the prospective linker the exact HTML code you want in the link and suggest which page you want the link from. This ensures the right words are used in the link and reduces the burden in setting up the link. Everybody on the internet is pressed for time and if you don't make it simple by giving them the exact HTML, you've made their job too hard. Make it easy and your success rate will go up.

Get directory listings

Jump-start your link campaign by getting directory links first; this is especially important if you have a new site or a site with no inbound links. A shortage of inbound links puts your site at a severe disadvantage because link analysis is an important part of every search engine's ranking algorithm. The way to overcome this is to get a few quality links. A good way to start is to get listed in as many directories as you can. There are many directories out there, and the more you can get into the better.

A few to target include:

1. Open Directory;
2. Yahoo!;
3. LookSmart;
4. Zeal.com;
5. Joeant.com;
6. Business.com.

Be aware that most of these directories (except the first one listed) require you to pay for a listing but it's worth the expense if you can afford it.

Consider bartering for links

It's a good idea to have something to offer in return for a link. Many sites won't link to you unless you link back to them or otherwise make it worth their while. Create a 'Resources' or 'Partner' page that allows you to have a place from which you can easily link to them. You might also offer to work a barter arrangement with them. If you have a site popular with their target market they might consider free advertisements in exchange for a link. If the link is of great value to you be prepared to give something back.

Link building alternative

If time constraints keep you from link building consider outsourcing your link popularity work. Link building is undoubtedly the most time consuming part of search engine optimisation. You may find it is not cost effective to do it yourself. That doesn't mean you shouldn't do it, it just means you hire someone else to do it for you.

Cautionary note: if you do chose to hire a company specialising in link building make sure they follow good link-building practices. Ask them to describe the process they use to request links. Make certain they follow a personalised approach and don't simply spam sites with requests for links. If they refuse to discuss their link building methods you can assume they use impersonal widespread email drops or link farms – that's spam. They may give it a sophisticated name, but if the process involves sending out large numbers of form emails, it's still spam and will only set your campaign backwards and injure your reputation. Go and find a different company or better still, develop the links you need yourself.

I've always done it; I've never spent a penny on the linking process.

Just do it!

Link popularity is important and the link-building process needs to be given high priority. Link analysis is only going to get more important to search engines, not less. Search engines have found it highly resistant to manipulation and a legitimate way to measure the importance of a site. Since link building takes time, the sooner you start the better.

So think of link building as a long-term investment in your site. Put in a little time now to improve your linking today to ensure a good search engine ranking in the future.

RECIPROCAL LINKING INCREASES WEBSITE EFFECTIVENESS

1. Other websites send you visitors because they link to you. If you have just 10 links pointing to your site and each site sends you on average only two visitors per day, you will only achieve 20 targeted prospects. Work at building your linking partners so that you attract much higher levels of targeted traffic.

2. Search engines like Google and Teoma use link popularity to rank websites. If your site has high link popularity then you will be rewarded with high rankings. To improve your link popularity you must have reciprocal links.

3. Exchanging reciprocal links with other sites in your niche will build a valuable links directory. Visitors will bookmark your website and visit you frequently because you can offer them a valuable resource: your links directory. The most frequented of my own pages is 'Resources' (see below) where my directory is located. My visitors love it and keep coming back for more.

Here is an example of a mini-site devoted entirely to reciprocal linking. I set it up in one hour some years ago and it still ranks at **No.2 out of 10,800,000** competitive pages on Yahoo!

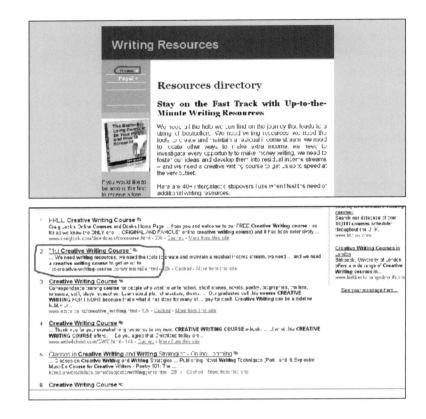

CREATE A TRAFFIC VIRUS BY COMBINING ARTICLES WITH LINKS

When you submit articles you are in effect setting up valuable links with the submission website centres and every time you submit to a new centre you are gaining a new link. Add to that the fact that the resource box in the articles contains your own website link. Tot it all up and what you have working for you is vital marketing and none of it is costing you anything but a little effort.

HOW TO GET BETTER THAN NO.1 ON GOOGLE

When you can arrange sponsorship tie-in links for your output (like the one below) **you rank above No.1** on the millions of free listings …

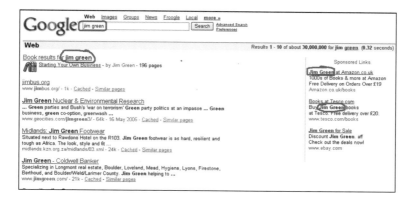

22
The changing face of email marketing

Until comparatively recent times email was the favourite tool of most online marketers; that is until the 'spammers' moved in and ruined it for everyone. Well, almost ruined it. You can still use email to great effect if you go about matters correctly. Spam (the odious practice of sending an email to thousands or even millions of people who have not requested it) is no longer tolerated. Nowadays offenders lose their local internet service provider, their websites, their email addresses, and more. Moreover, email server systems such as Yahoo! and Hotmail use highly sophisticated filters which weed out the bad boys and ban them outright.

THE CONTROVERSY SURROUNDING BULK EMAIL

Don't even think about using bulk email; just one complaint (which you will get even if you try to hide) and your server will cancel your account.

And yet some reckless fruitcakes persist in bulk emailing even though they run the gauntlet every time they do it. Why do they persist? They look at it this way: although the response rates are extremely low, they still do manage to get a trickle of orders for their products and services – *for the time being*, but not for long.

THERE IS A BETTER, LEGITIMATE WAY: OPT-IN EMAIL

Opt-in email works like this. You invite people to join your email list and you can do that in several acceptable ways.

- Through your website;

- Through subscriptions to your newsletter (which we'll cover in the next chapter);

- Through giving away free information produce.

All three of these options can operate in tandem. When visitors enter your site you capture their attention with an internal pop-up window or a carefully worded panel requesting them to subscribe to your newsletter. To qualify they must provide you with a current email address which gives you permission to contact them in future. Equally, to receive an ebook you give away for free, visitors must once again provide you with a legitimate email address and so you get the contact, they get the freebie: simple but highly effective and legal.

COMMON EXCUSES FOR NOT IMPLEMENTING OPT-IN EMAIL

Many marketers never get around to implementing an opt-in email system because ...

'I can't be bothered' – You should: take the trouble to set up your own opt-in email system without delay. Email is free and when used correctly it leads to sales. If you elect not to participate you are leaving money on the table because by far the majority of online sales do not emanate directly from websites; they come from lists; lists of people who have given you permission to contact them; lists of people who have already purchased from you.

'I wouldn't know how' – It's as simple as falling off a log when you employ the avenues listed above.

'I couldn't come up with content for a newsletter' – Yes, you could. You have all the necessary material to hand in the articles you have already prepared and are continuing to write for distribution purposes.

It just takes a little extra effort from you to set up and include them in your own newsletter.

'I won't be starting a newsletter; there are too many out there already' – Oh, yes? Newsletters come and go, that's for sure, but the quality sheets go from strength to strength. If you don't fancy the standard format why not come up with something different? Like 'My Recipe for Today', 'My Marketing Tip for Today' or a newsletter in the form of an ongoing daily diary of how you are developing your enterprise? What about a free online class? You could develop a 6-, 12-, 24-lesson class on your topic and have subscribers receive the next issue every week, every 2 weeks, or once a month. Then, once they complete that class, you introduce advanced classes, etc. You could also put your subscribers on an updates list for new information constantly. Put your thinking cap on and create some ideas of your own before you ditch the notion of a newsletter.

'I don't see the point in giving stuff away for free' – If you can't see the point, flick forward to Chapter 27 for enlightenment.

12 COMMON EMAIL MISTAKES YOU MUST AVOID AT ALL COSTS

People make these mistakes all the time when using email and it costs them; they lose out on credibility. Don't allow that to happen to you in your online marketing.

1. **Omitting the subject line**
   Gone are the days when email users didn't realise the significance of the subject line. It makes no sense to send a message that reads 'No Subject' and seems to be about nothing of any consequence. Given the volume of email that everyone receives, the subject header is essential if you want your message read. The subject line has become the hook.

2. **Not making the subject content meaningful**
   Your header should be pertinent to the message. The recipient is

going to decide the order in which he/she reads email based on who sent it and what it is about. Your virtual messages have lots of competition. If you want to interest recipients in a 'Great New Marketing Breakthrough', tell them so in the header.

3. **Failing to change the header to correspond with the subject**
For example, if you are writing to your web publisher, your first header may be 'Website Content'. However, as your site develops and you send more information, label each message for what it is, 'Contact Info', 'Graphics', or 'Home Page'. Adding more details to the header will allow the recipient to find a specific document in their message folder without having to search every one you sent. Start a new message if you change the subject altogether.

4. **Failing to personalise the message**
Email is informal but it still needs a greeting. Begin with 'Dear Mr. Broome', 'Dear Jim', 'Hello Jim', or just 'Jim'. Failure to insert the recipient's name can make you and your email seem cold.

5. **Not accounting for 'tone'**
When you communicate with another person face to face, 93 per cent of the message is non-verbal. Email has no body language. The reader cannot see your face or hear your tone of voice, so choose your words carefully and thoughtfully. Put yourself in the other person's place and think how your words may come across on the internet.

6. **Forgetting to check for spelling and grammar**
In the early days of email someone created the notion that this form of communication did not have to be letter perfect. Wrong! It does. It is a representation of you and your enterprise. If you don't check to be sure email is correct, people will question the calibre of other work you do. Use proper capitalisation and punctuation, and always check your spelling. Remember that your spellchecker will catch misspelled words, but not misused ones. It cannot tell whether you meant to say 'from' or 'form',

'for' or 'fro', 'he' or 'the'.

7. **Composing an epic**

   Email is meant to be brief. Keep your message short. Use only a few paragraphs and a few sentences per paragraph. People skim, so a long missive is wasted. If you find yourself writing an overly long message, start editing down.

8. **Forwarding email without permission**

   If the message was sent to you and only you, why would you take responsibility for passing it on? Too often confidential information has gone global because of someone's lack of judgment. Unless you are asked or request permission do not forward anything that was sent just to you.

9. **Assuming that no one else will ever see your email**

   Once it has left your mailbox you have no idea where your email will end up. Don't use the internet to send anything that you couldn't stand to see on a local billboard. Use other means to communicate personal or sensitive information.

10. **Omitting your signature**

    Always close with your name, even though it is included at the top of the message and add contact information such as your phone, fax and street address. The recipient may want to call to talk further or send you documents that cannot be emailed. Creating a formal signature block with all that data is the most professional approach.

11. **Expecting an instant response**

    Not everyone is sitting in front of the computer with email turned on. The beauty of an internet communication is that it is convenient. It is not an interruption. People can check their messages when it suits them, not you. If your communication is so important that you need to hear back right away, use the phone.

12. **Completing the 'to' line first**

    The name or address of the person to whom you are writing is actually the last piece of information you should enter. Check everything else over carefully first; proof for grammar, punctuation, spelling and clarity. Did you say what needed to be said? How was your 'tone'? If you were the least bit emotional when you wrote the email, did you let it sit for a period of time? Did you include the attachment you wanted to send? If you enter the recipient's name first, a mere slip of the finger can send a message before its time. You can never take it back.

12 CARELESS PRACTICES THAT SABOTAGE EMAIL MARKETING

1. **Don't load the copy, push 'send' and move on**
   We've all got a lot on our plates and it's easy to be trigger-happy with the send button. Have you received emails with misspellings or odd formatting? It makes you think twice about the sender.

   Take time to proof your emails before they go out. Run a spell-checker, and make sure the format looks the way you expected it to in the top email clients (e.g., AOL, Outlook, Eudora). Also, review list selection and verify any personalisation rules.

2. **Don't include lots of broken links**
   Broken links are a major cause of reduced response. A study by email marketing software and services firm Silverpop found nearly half of all emails contain errors such as broken graphics or raw HTML code. Even when earlier versions of AOL and Lotus Notes (which has always been problematic) are eliminated from results, more than 18 per cent of HTML emails had some rendering problem.

   Set up test accounts with the major online services and see for yourself how your campaigns display.

3. **Don't ignore spam filters**
   The deliverability maze can be so overwhelming that it's tempting to just ignore the topic. If your messages don't get

through they can't drive revenue. Use a content checker to scan your subject line and body copy to improve the odds that your mail won't be filtered out. Most email service bureaus offer built-in content checkers. Plus, there are also free online resources to test your message before it goes out. This is the content checker I use: http://spamcheck.sitesell.com.
Submit test versions of your email, and this service will provide a free evaluation of your campaign and indicate what might trigger a filter.

4. **Don't ignore your bounces**
   Today's internet service providers (ISPs) are very demanding and one area of focus is undeliverable email coming from individual marketers. If you exceed their standards for undeliverable or bounced messages, they may flag you as a spammer and your mail may be blocked.

   There's some good news on this front. Email marketing and online advertising firm *DoubleClick* has done an excellent job at monitoring quarterly trends and publishing the results on its site. The firm's latest report shows bounce rates across its client base have declined to 11.5 per cent. But that's still high!
   Establish thresholds for re-mailing both hard and soft bounces and retire email addresses after threshold limits are exceeded.

5. **Don't capture several pages of data during registration**
   Direct marketers are data junkies and it's tempting to want to know everything possible about online registrants. Have you ever been intrigued by an offer, yet abandoned the sign-up process when you were asked too many questions?
   Short registration forms work, and you can still ask qualifying questions. Make it easy to complete, and don't ask for information you're not going to use. An important metric to examine is the abandonment rate for your sign-up forms.

6. **Don't design an email program without looking at the website**
   An email recipient may click on a beautifully crafted email and

be brought to a landing page or micro site that has a totally different look and feel. This is especially true if you're doing affiliate work. Remember the best user experience is a seamless one. Your emails should be consistent with the site you're promoting.

7. **Don't select rental email lists based on price**
   There are inexpensive cost-per-action (CPA) lists available. Marketers pay only for those recipients who meet performance criteria set in advance: clicks, registrations or purchases. On the surface this sounds like a great deal: you control your marketing costs and pay only if someone responds. Be wary though. Many CPA lists simply blast all names on the list rather than use selection criteria. Also, the level of permission may be suspect. Use these lists and you run the risk of being labelled a spammer.

   Work with a quality e-list broker who provides information such as prior usage and how the individuals opted in. Expect that most good lists only will be available on a cost-per-thousand basis.

8. **Don't keep your list size up by making it hard to opt out**
   Some marketers ask you to reply to a message and include 'remove me' or 'unsubscribe' in the subject line. The theory behind this is that more people will stay on the list. But this practice reduces the effectiveness of the list. Communicate with recipients who welcome your message and you will have better results.

9. **Don't sell, sell, sell ...**
   E-commerce marketers want to monetise their efforts by selling goods and services. It's tempting to fill every inch of your emails with product offerings.

   The best email plans have a balance between selling and content. The content can provide behind-the-scenes information about products, tell a story about your company, or provide tips and hints on how customers use a product.

Value-added content will keep your recipients interested.

10. Don't think online only

The beauty of email is that it's a great way to promote your offer and drive traffic right to your content. However, customers or prospects may not want to order online. Don't think only in one dimension.

Provide ways for recipients to contact you offline by including your toll-free number both in emails and on your site. Some marketers have measured the impact of including their 0800 number in emails and found up to 20 per cent of sales came in through the call centre.

11. Don't forget to make time to test or measure

Testing and analysis take time, and time always seems to be in short supply. If you approach each email as a one-time event that lives or dies based on results, you never will achieve all that you could.

A plan with specific goals will provide you with a road map to success. Testing is relatively easy in email. Create hypotheses and test to see if you're right. Build upon your previous efforts in terms of what worked and what didn't work. Your campaigns should be interconnected.

12. Don't assume offline customers would have registered if they wanted to receive emails

This may be true for a percentage of your customers, but there are many who simply haven't thought to sign up. Email appending works for many marketers who want to further penetrate their customer database. Select a quality supplier with a database that clearly is permission-based. Take the time to nurture any names with a special plan.

Obviously, no one would deliberately sabotage an email campaign. Consider this food for thought to help maximise your efforts.

FIVE WAYS TO EARN MORE USING EMAIL

Use this short checklist to ensure that you are taking full advantage of the power of email and by so doing, making time your ally, not your adversary. Fast, easy, and free, the consistent use of email in the following areas will yield powerful results for you.

1. **Customer follow-up**

   Whether it's a simple as a one-time 'thank you' or as elaborate as a 50-message follow up system, customers love to know you care. At a minimum, send one message thanking customers for every order.

2. **Customer learning**

   Do you offer a product that takes a bit of learning to use? Teach your customers how to get the benefits they deserve from your product or service via email. Keep messages on topic and separate your follow-up series into bite-size learning pieces. These follow-up messages can bring your refund rate to near zero.

3. **Pre-sales series**

   How often do you buy the first thing you see? Comparison shopping is the way of the internet and getting prospective customers to return to your site is the challenge. A pre-sale series is the answer and it's very easy to do. Just write down the top ten reasons why someone should buy from you, then put each in a follow-up message. Send one a day until they are all delivered. Offer the series to everyone who visits your site and let time do the selling work for you. My experience has been that up to 40 per cent of visitors will take your free information if you do a good job of selling the idea.

4. **Special pricing and offers**

   Use email to deliver insider information on special bargains, limited time pricing, and more. Much like a coupon sheet in your local newspaper, selling advertising in this type of email is a breeze.

5. Hard-to-find news

People love offbeat news, especially when it has a connection to their lives.

For an example of this technique visit this website www.thisistrue.com. You'll love it!

MORE IDEAS ON HOW TO USE EMAIL TO SELL MORE

1. Announce special events.

2. Do a joint venture (JV) with someone whose product complements your own.

3. Sell a message in your follow-up series.

4. Teach affiliates how to sell more for you.

5. Create a discussion to do research for your next product.

EMAIL MAKES EVERYTHING EASIER AND FASTER

It creates a powerful commercial impression and establishes positive professional relationships. The small business entrepreneur who uses the technology effectively and appropriately will see the results of that effort reflected in the bottom line.

23

Why you must create your own newsletter

So, you've decided to start a newsletter? I'm glad to hear it. You are about to embark on a very exciting and rewarding venture – watching your online publication grow, trying out new tactics to attract subscribers, even making some money. It becomes addictive. You'll see why as you progress …

THE GOALS ALL NEWSLETTER PUBLISHERS STRIVE TO ACHIEVE

1. They all want increased subscriptions.

2. They all want increased exposure.

Driving subscriptions and enhancing the profile of your newsletter are the core activities for success. There are 300,000+ other newsletters competing for the same subscribers, so the better you become at chasing your goals, the faster you will succeed. Gaining momentum is the hardest part. Where do you begin in your quest for say, 10,000 subscribers and maximum exposure?

Key no. 1: Submit to Newsletter Directories

Before you jump in though: have another look at the description you have created for your newsletter. With so many ezines already out there, what is going to make yours stand out from the rest?

- If I were glancing over 100+ ezines in your category, why would I choose yours?

- Your description is a key element to attracting new subscribers and so it's a good practice to study other ezine descriptions before creating your own. Visit a few of the top directories and search through various newsletters in the same category as your own.

Here are a few websites to get you started:

www.ezineaction.com
www.ezineadvertising.com
www.ezine-dir.com
www.ezinelocater.com
www.ezine-marketing.com
www.ezinesearch.com
www.ezinesplus.com
www.ezinestoday.com
http://ezinearticles.com
http://new-list.com

Take note of which descriptions catch your eye. Which jump out at you? Which are as dull as ditch water? www.e-zines.com is a great site to get up to speed on writing good descriptions.

Here's an example of a good description …

'Powerful internet marketing concepts that you can use right now; informative articles written by professional marketers who make their living online, money making tips and tricks you must use to increase your profits, and much more! Receive 4 free gifts when you subscribe!'

Here's an example of a poor description …

'An electronic newsletter especially created to help new and/or frustrated internet marketers prosperously market online.'

See the difference? They're both internet marketing newsletters. Which one would you subscribe to?

Once you have studied competitive descriptions, develop a few of your own. Then pick the best one.

CORE INCENTIVE TO SUBMIT YOUR NEWSLETTER TO THE DIRECTORIES

In a concerted effort to increase search engine ranking most of these directories submit their website on a regular basis. And guess what? Your newsletter title will also start showing up in the major engines – increasing exposure even further.

Key no. 2: Announce Your Ezine Through Announcement Lists

Announcement Lists are extremely powerful. When used correctly they have the potential to bring in 500–700 subscribers in a single week. What are Announcement Lists? They are mailing lists that are dedicated to announcing new newsletters on a daily or weekly basis. Most of them will allow you to announce your ezine including your description and subscription information.

Here's a short list to get you started:

List Builder:
List_Builder-subscribe@topica.com

1 List Advertising:
http://groups.yahoo.com

A Announce:
http://groups.yahoo.com

Add Your List:
http://groups.yahoo.com

Key no. 3: Use The Power of Free Ads

Using free ads is nothing new but don't underestimate them; they constitute a powerful tool to have in your marketing arsenal. There are two basic types: free and swaps. How do swaps work? It's pretty obvious. You contact ezine publishers and approach them about exchanging ads. There's a catch with free ads – most of them include other people's ads and as a result are not as potent as swaps. You'll need an auto-responder for both types and here are some suggestions:

www.aweber.com
www.getresponse.com
www.autobots.net
www.autoresponders.com
www.freeautobot.com
www.ultimateresponse.com

You don't need to waste time submitting your ads manually. Here's a piece of software that lets you blast out hundreds of free ads and ad swap requests with a few clicks of your mouse. It also includes over 275 ad swap sources and 100+ free ad sources with tracking capabilities built into the software. To download a trial version, click on the following link:

www.articleannouncer.com

Key no. 4 – Let Your Articles Auto-Promote Your Ezine

Writing articles for other ezines may be the most effective and easiest way to market your newsletter. In fact, some successful publishers use articles as their only source of promotion. You already know the drill. You learned it in Chapter 20 …

Key no. 5: Exchange Links With Similar Ezines/Websites.

Here's a little story I heard recently and it's true …

A group of local fast-food restaurant owners were complaining about the lack of business. One of them had a bizarre idea. He approached three of his competitors and asked whether they would promote his restaurant if he did the same for theirs. The fish & chip, pizza, and burger restaurants all began to promote each other. Guess what happened? Everyone's business increased. This technique will also work for you when you link to other related newsletters and websites.

SECRETS THAT CONVERT YOUR NEWSLETTER INTO A CASH MACHINE

Secret no. 1: Your Subscriber List Is Everything To You

Your emailing list is central to everything connected with your online activity. It needs to be made up of good quality recipients and ideally it needs to be quite big. Most important of all, you must take the time and trouble to look after the subscribers who have graced your list by signing up of their own volition.

Let me give you a couple of examples ...

Make plain your publishing intention and stick to it

If you advertise that you intend to send out your newsletter on a Wednesday, stick with that schedule. Random editions sent when your recipients are least expecting them might draw them to suspect that you are running a slap-dash venture. If they think that your offerings are less than professional then they'll probably migrate to one of your competitors.

Never endorse a product you haven't tried or don't like

You want to make money from your newsletter and that's good. But make sure that you are providing your readers with pure quality. Resist the ever-present temptation to recommend and endorse a product simply because the vendor is running an affiliate programme paying you out a high percentage of the sale proceeds. You might make a few extra pounds in the short term, but it'll cost you subscribers (that's money too) in the longer run by destroying trust between you and your readers.

So treat your readers like Kings and Queens. Never abuse their trust and work to build their loyalty. Remember: Your subscriber list is everything to you …

Secret no. 2: Brainstorming for the Perfect Newsletter Topic

First of all you must acknowledge that the list of possible newsletter topics is virtually endless. You don't need to be the editor of yet another publication spouting on about how to make money on the internet. That is what almost everyone else does. Try brainstorming to uncover an offbeat, wacky topic. For instance, would you consider producing a newsletter that sends jokes to its readers on a daily basis? You wouldn't make money from it, right? Wrong. Someone does. His name is Ray Owens. He set up the 'Joke-A-Day' ezine and is reported to have pulled in £85,000 revenue in the process through selling advertising and merchandise in the past year alone …
The key advantage of an online newsletter over conventional publishing is the ability to speak to a tiny niche section, even just a subsection of an interested group of people.

Think of the possibilities...

> **TIP**
>
> The 'Easy Ezine Toolkit' spells out how to brainstorm for the perfect money-making newsletter topic and how to test market your shortlist to discover which subject will bring you the most subscribers flooding in, just pleading to get their hands on your ezine. If that sounds good to you, head over to this site now www.howtocorp.com/sales.php?offer=writing333&pid=6 and

get instant access to the web's best ezine creator toolkit. I use it – and so should you if you want your newsletter to be both original and successful.

24
The influence of list building in attracting prospects

There's an oft-quoted saying among successful e-entrepreneurs: '*The money is in the list*'. And so it is. More sales are generated from quality lists than from any other online marketing activity. Build a list of targeted contacts for your business – and sales will come. I can't think of anyone better to convince you of the power of building an opt-in list than my online friend Shelley Lowery. Shelley is a hands-on expert and her own list at web-source.net is well into six figures. She recently produced a cutting edge article on the subject and has kindly given me permission to reproduce it here.

About the Author: Shelley Lowery is the author of the acclaimed web design course *Web Design Mastery* www.webdesignmastery.com and ebook Starter – *Give Your Ebooks the Look and Feel of a Real Book* www.ebookstarter.com. Visit Web-Source.net to sign up for a complimentary subscription to Etips and receive a copy of the acclaimed ebook *Killer Internet Marketing Strategies*.

SECRETS TO BUILDING MASSIVE OPT-IN LISTS

An opt-in list is the absolute most effective marketing tool available on the internet. Not only does it provide you with a direct line of communication with your target market, it also enables you to develop a trusting relationship with your subscribers.

The key to using an opt-in list effectively is to develop a large subscriber base. If you've struggled with increasing your subscriber base this article will reveal some of the most effective methods used to build an opt-in list. If you're not using these methods you're losing hundreds of new subscribers each week.

If you really want to build a massive list you must provide your potential subscribers with an incentive. Competition on the internet is fierce. You can no longer simply tell visitors what your publication will provide and expect a large percentage to subscribe. It simply won't work.

There are thousands of publications online and most of your visitors are probably already subscribed to many. Why would they want to subscribe to another one? Sure, you'll get some new subscribers, but how many? Enough to build a massive opt-in list? The truth is, if you continue to build your list simply by displaying a sign-up box on your site and listing your publication at the listing sites it will take years to develop a substantial list. You must give your visitors a reason to subscribe.

Incentives

Using incentives is a highly effective method of obtaining new subscribers. However, they must be of value and of interest to your target audience.

Some popular incentives include:

- Exclusive ebooks that provide valuable information that will be of interest to your target market.

- Special reports that provide exclusive, detailed information in regard to a specific subject.

- Special software programs that will assist your visitors.

If you're not comfortable developing your own incentives there are hundreds of great ebooks available online that you may freely distribute. You can find some here: www.web-source.net/free_ebooks.htm.

Subscription exchange incentives

In addition to using incentives to gain new subscribers you can also use a subscription exchange. In exchange for your visitor's subscription, you could provide any of the following:

- Provide access to a 'members only' area of your website.

- Provide a service.

- List their website within your directory or integral search engine.

In order for your visitors to use your services they agree to receive your publication.

Popup windows

Although popup windows can be irritating if not used correctly they provide a highly effective means of obtaining new subscribers. The key to using popup windows effectively is to combine them with your incentives.

Design a small popup window that utilises 'cookies' and only displays the first time your visitor enters your site. This window should contain information about your publication and incentive. It might read something like this:

'Subscribe to A1 Marketing Tips and receive a copy of the highly acclaimed ebook, Secrets of the Internet Marketing Gurus completely free.'

Your subscription box should follow this sentence.

You can find a nice popup script that utilises cookies here:

www.web-source.net/javascript_popup_window3.htm

You can find a complete list of sites offering free scripts here:

www.web-source.net/web/JavaScripts/

Alert boxes

Although using popup windows with incentives is a highly effective method of obtaining new subscribers there is one other method that is even better. When combined with an incentive this method will literally double your subscriptions instantly. It's similar to a popup window but it doesn't require your visitor to fill out a form.

When a visitor enters your site an alert box will appear. This alert box should display text requesting their subscription and information about your incentive. Your visitor can choose to click on 'OK' to subscribe or 'Cancel' to close the alert.

The alert box is displayed via a script that extracts your visitor's name and email address. If they choose to subscribe it then sends their subscription request, via email, to your subscription address and adds it to your database. In addition, you can send personalised messages to your subscribers; use auto-responder follow-ups and provide your subscribers with 'one click' unsubscribe links within your messages.

To increase your subscriptions even further you can also place a subscription box on each page of your website.

For further information, visit:

www.web-source.net/

Conclusion

No matter how many new subscribers you may acquire, the key to a successful opt-in list is keeping them. The relationship you build with your subscribers will determine your success. Above all, you must provide your readers with quality content. They subscribed to your publication for a reason. If it doesn't meet their expectations they'll simply unsubscribe.

Once you've developed a trusting relationship with your subscribers, your personal recommendations will be a very effective method of closing sales. However, it is very important that you only recommend a product or service that you truly believe in. Your professional reputation depends on it.

Copyright © Shelley Lowery

www.web-source.net

I have personally learned more from Shelley Lowery on the subject of opt-in list building than from any other leading online marketer.

TIP

Shelley Lowery is masterful in the art of building massive opt-in lists. Emulate her strategies and you will make rapid inroads on creating your own lists of eager subscribers.

25

Create your own blog and send business messages to the world

A blog is a personal diary; a daily pulpit; a collaborative space; a political soapbox; a breaking-news outlet; a collection of links. In effect, a blog is the online transmission of your own private thoughts and memos to the world.

Your blog is whatever you want it to be; there are millions of them, in all shapes and sizes, and there are no real rules. While it is not essential to have one, it could nevertheless provide a useful adjunct to your online strategy.

In simple terms, a blog is a website where you write stuff on an ongoing basis. New stuff shows up at the top so that your visitors can read what's topical. Then they comment on it or link to it or email you – or not.

Since Blogger.com was launched almost five years ago blogs have reshaped the web, impacted politics, shaken up journalism, and enabled millions of people to have a voice and connect with others.

And yet the whole concept is just getting started.

PUBLISH YOUR THOUGHTS

A blog gives you your own voice on the web. It is a place to collect and share things that you find interesting – whether it is your personal diary on matters of interest in your field of operation, or links to websites you want to remember.

Many people use a blog just to organise their own thoughts while others command influential, worldwide audiences of thousands. Professional and amateur journalists use blogs to publish breaking news, while commercial journal makers reveal inner thoughts on what's happening in their chosen business sector.

Whatever you have to say, Blogger can help you say it.

GET FEEDBACK

The blogging experience is about not only putting your thoughts on the web, but also about hearing back from, and connecting with, other like-minded enthusiasts.

- *Blogger Comments* let readers of your site from all over the world give feedback on what you share on your blog. You can choose whether or not you want to allow comments on a post-by-post basis (and you can delete anything you do not like).

- *Group blogs* can be excellent communication tools for small business teams; consider giving your team its own space on the web for sharing news, links, and ideas.

- *Blogger Profiles* let you find people and blogs that share your interests. And your profile lets people find you (but only if you want to be found).

- *Blogger Profile* lists your blogs, your recent posts and more. Clicking on interests or location takes you to other people's profiles whose blogs you might enjoy.

POST PHOTOS

Sometimes you just want to share a product photo (there is a button for uploading photos in the Blogger interface). Just click the photo button to upload a photo from your computer. If the image you would like to put on your blog is already on the web that's okay too. Just tell Blogger.com where it is.

You can also upload images by attaching them to any email sent to your own mail-to-blogger address. And you can send camera phone photos straight to your blog while you are on-the-go with Blogger Mobile.

GO MOBILE

Blogger Mobile lets you send photos and text straight to your blog while you are on-the-go. All you need to do is send a message to go@blogger.com from your phone. You do not even need a Blogger account. The message itself is enough to create a brand new blog and post whatever photo and text you have sent.

Later, if you want to claim your mobile blog or switch your posts to another blog, just sign in to go.blogger.com and use the claim code Blogger sent to your phone.

While Blogger Mobile is currently only available in the US, you can always send posts to your blog using Mail-to-Blogger.

There is even a feature called AudioBlogger that lets you call Blogger from any phone and leave a message that is immediately posted to your site as an MP3 audio file.

GETTING STARTED

The fastest way to understand blogging is to try it out. You will find easy-to-follow instructions at the website; instructions that are so simple, you will have created your first blog in minutes.

And remember, Blogger is totally free. In the unlikely event you encounter teething problems just click the 'Help' button from any screen and you can find the answer that you are looking for – or ask support staff for assistance.

Sign up for free at www.blogger.com and start your own small business blog straightaway.

> ### TIP
>
> When you are up and running with your own blog, visit this website www.pingomatic.com and use the software for free. This is an automated tool to submit your blogs to over 30 blog search engines with just one click. Pinging your blogs to the search engines is the fastest way to get the search engine robots to visit your blog and gain increased traffic in a short amount of time.

26
What RSS is and what it can do for you

Hard on the heels of blogging comes RSS (a family of XML file formats for web syndication used by news websites and weblogs) which although around since 1997, only gained media attention in 2004. Simply put, it is a straightforward technology for sharing and distributing stuff like data, news headlines and other web page content with other webmasters and users – and now more and more people are embracing RSS just like the time when email was first introduced.

BRAND NEW, UNTAPPED MARKETING CHANNEL

RSS is rapidly becoming the preferred method of distributing news and information online and informed users are subscribing to RSS feeds to read news online and to receive updates from their favourite publishers.

WHAT IT MEANS FOR YOU

It's a brand new marketing channel to promote your products; a channel with enormous potential.

ELIMINATE THE SPAM FILTER NUISANCE

Spam is one of the biggest headaches faced by every online marketer. Email marketing is getting harder with each passing day. It is reported that as much as 38 per cent of all emails are being filtered by over-zealous ISPs.

You may have thousands of subscribers but only a handful is receiving your messages.

WHAT CAN YOU DO?

RSS provides an elegant solution. Send all your marketing messages, follow-ups and promotions directly to your subscribers desktop. No need to worry about spam complaints, filters, and the like.

DOES IT SOUND TOO GOOD TO BE TRUE?

Let me assure you, it's all true.

RSS is still in its infancy but it won't remain that way for long. Do a search for *email* on Google and you come up with 290 million results; do a search for *RSS* – only 41 million results.

When Microsoft's support for RSS is finalised for Windows software, everyone will know about RSS. Over 90 per cent of all PCs connected to the internet are using Microsoft's Windows software.

- Do you want to be a pioneer and profit from RSS?

- Or will you wait and watch as your competitors leave you in the dust?

THE MAJORITY OF THE ONLINE MARKETERS HAVE NEVER HEARD OF RSS

Their ignorance is to your advantage. Some have heard of RSS but ignored it. Some scratched their heads, trying to figure out what the fuss is all about...

HERE'S WHAT RSS CAN DO FOR YOU IN A NUTSHELL

- Get your site listed in Yahoo!'s latest RSS directory for free right now. This may not last forever as Yahoo! is currently on a blitz to populate their RSS directory. Once they have sufficient RSS feeds (contents), this window of opportunity may be closed forever. Why pay when you can be listed for free now?

- Update your websites with fresh, relevant contents – automatically – without writing a single word. Google loves sites that are updated daily. The spiders usually crawl twice a month – at the beginning and at the end of each month. But if your sites are updated daily with fresh contents, Google will come almost daily.

- RSS allows you to tell the world, and more importantly, the search engine spiders that you've updated your websites.

- Bait the search engine spiders and get them to crawl your site whenever you've added new contents. Why wait until the end of the month or the beginning of the month?

- RSS gives you a brand new, untapped marketing channel to display your ads, messages, and news directly onto your subscribers desktop.

- Many online marketers are still oblivious to this emerging marketing tool. You can leapfrog over them right now.

- Over-zealous ISPs can blacklist your host because you send too many emails messages/RSS provides the perfect solution.

- Get other webmasters to carry your articles, your messages on their websites without it costing you a penny (and you won't have tediously to submit your articles either).

Imagine hundreds of other websites carrying your news and articles – imagine the extra exposure you will receive. What an incredible tool to build your credibility and brand name online – effortlessly.

TIP

You can get up to speed on RSS by investing $30.97 (approx. £22.60) in Adrian Ling's new product *RSS Made Easy* at www.rss-made-easy.com/launch.html.

27
Let Google Adsense add to your online income

Google AdSense is the programme that can generate advertising revenue from each page on your small business website – with no financial outlay, minimal investment in time, and no additional resources; a free way to add to your online income.

DISCOVER YOUR SITE'S FULL REVENUE POTENTIAL

It's a fast and easy way for website publishers of all sizes to display relevant Google ads on their website's content pages and earn money. Because the ads are related to what your visitors are looking for on your site – or matched to the characteristics and interests of the visitors your content attracts – you'll finally have a way to both capitalise on and enhance your content pages.

It's also a way for website publishers to provide Google web and site search to their visitors and to earn money by displaying Google ads on the search results pages.

PRECISELY TARGETED TO YOUR WEBSITE CONTENT

AdSense delivers relevant text and image ads that are precisely targeted to your site and its content. And when you add a Google search box, AdSense delivers relevant text ads that are targeted to the Google search results pages generated by your visitors' search request.

MAXIMISE REVENUE POTENTIAL BY DISPLAYING GOOGLE ADS ON YOUR WEBSITE

Google puts relevant CPC (cost-per-click) and CPM (cost per thousand impressions) ads through the same auction, and lets them compete against one another. The auction takes place instantaneously and when it's over, AdSense automatically displays the text or image ad(s) that will generate the maximum revenue for a page – and the maximum revenue for you.

BECOMING AN ADSENSE PUBLISHER IS SIMPLE

All it takes is a single online application. Once you're approved, AdSense takes only minutes to set up. Just copy and paste a block of HTML and targeted ads start showing up on your website.

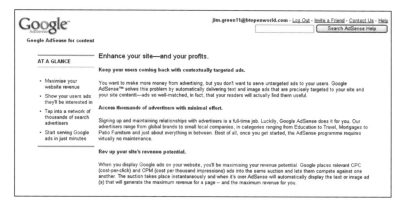

ADSENSE TAKES THE STING OUT OF ONLINE ADVERTISING

The extensive database provides:

• Ads for every category of enterprise;

• All types of content no matter how broad or specialised.

And because you are working with a composite format, you do not need to maintain individual advertiser relationships.

FROM LOCAL TO GLOBAL

The Google Adsense marketing strategy focuses on geographical targeting:

- You can stay local and advertise to your immediate marketplace;
- You can go global if you wish and advertise your wares to an international audience.

You can even couch your message in a variety of languages ...

SMART TECHNOLOGY MEANS SMARTER ADVERTISING

Words can have several different meanings, depending on context. Google technology grasps these distinctions; so you get more targeted ads.

GOOGLE'S AD REVIEW PROCESS ENSURES STRICT SECURITY

The process combines sensitive language filters and a team of linguists automatically to filter out ads that may be inappropriate for your content. Furthermore, you can block competitive ads and choose your own default ads.

CUSTOMISE THE APPEARANCE OF YOUR ADS

You can customise the appearance of ads; choosing from a wide range of colours and templates. You can do the same with your search results page. Your reports can be customised too. Flexible reporting tools let you group your pages in any way you want so you can view your results by URL, domain, ad type, category and more to learn where your earnings are coming from.

RUN ADSENSE ON ALL OR JUST SELECTED PAGES

You can run Google ads on all or just some of your pages; using AdSense strategically to complement marketing. You will pay nothing, spend little time on set-up, and have no maintenance worries. You can use AdSense for a day, a month or for however long it pleases you to make a profit – you choose.

PLACE A GOOGLE SEARCH BOX ON YOUR SITE

When you place a Google search box on your site you can start capitalising on the results from web searches. Not only does this keep your users on your website longer – since they can search from where they are – it takes just minutes to implement. And you pay nothing to participate.

You are in control from start to finish.

TIP

Do as I do and use and Google Adsense on your site(s). Sign up for free at www.google.com/adsense and inject an automatic supplementary income-generating tool to your small business online marketing programme.

28
Converting prospects into customers

You have come a long way in the development of your online marketing programme, but to make it profitable your focus must always be on converting prospects into cash-paying customers. Mastering the basics – creating ideas, turning them into produce, and learning how to promote isn't enough. These are just the tools to get you moving. Now you must drive the engine. Let's look at the buying process from the flipside: why prospects won't buy from you when you fail to appreciate the rules of converting them into customers.

PEOPLE WON'T BUY FROM YOU IF YOU MAKE ANY OF THESE MISTAKES

Here are ten simple yet powerful ideas for you to reflect on. They will help you adjust your marketing strategies on everything you sell.

1 – You don't make people feel safe when they order

Remind people that they are ordering through a secure server. Tell them you won't sell their email address and all their information will be kept confidential.

2 – You don't make your ad copy attractive

Your ad lists features instead of benefits. The headline does not attract your target audience. You don't list any testimonials or guarantees in your ad.

3 – You don't remind people to come back and visit

People usually don't purchase the first time they visit. The more times they visit your site, the greater the chance they will buy. The most effective way is to give them a free subscription to your newsletter.

4 – You don't let people know anything about your business

They will feel more comfortable if they know who they are buying from. Publish a section entitled 'About Us' on your website. Include your profile, contact information, etc.

5 – You don't give people as many ordering options as possible

Accept credit cards, cheques, money orders, and other forms of electronic payments. Take orders by phone, email, website, fax, mail, etc.

6 – You don't make your website look professional

You must have your own domain name. Your website should be easy to navigate through. The graphics should be related to the theme of your site.

7 – You don't let people read your ad before they get your freebie

When you use free stuff to lure people to your website include the reference below your ad copy or on another web page. If you list the freebie above your ad they may never look to see what you're selling.

8 – You don't attract the target audience that would buy your product or service

A simple way to check on this is to survey your existing customers to see what attracted them to buy. This information will help you improve your target marketing and advertising.

9 – You don't test and improve your ad copy

Many people never change their ad copy. You have to test frequently and improve to get the highest possible response rate.

10 – You don't give people any urgency to buy

Some prospects are interested in your product, but they are put off buying it until later and eventually forget about it. Entice them to buy now with a freebie or discount and include a deadline date when the offer ends.

BE AWARE OF THE GOLDEN RULE OF SELLING ONLINE

You will never actually *sell* anything to anyone at any time – but they might just buy from you ...

1. If you are operating in the same marketplace as your prospects.

2. If you respect their intelligence.

3. If you are honest with them.

4. If you give them good reason to trust you.

5. If you know what it is they want.

6. If you can provide a genuine solution.

7. If your produce does all you say it will do.

8. If you can back up your claims with unsolicited testimonials.

9. If you can offer a guarantee.

10. If you make it easy for your prospects to pay you.

TIP

Complete compliance with points 2–10 won't amount to a row of beans if you miss the target on Point No. 1. Shout as hard and as long as you want in the marketplace, but make sure it's the right marketplace …

29
How to set up an online payment system

If you fail to set up a system to accept credit cards at your website (which you can do without obtaining merchant status) you will not get many sales. However, before we launch into a review of credit card processing systems it is worth noting that despite growing universal usage there is still uneasiness among consumers about disclosing credit card details online. The following extract from a survey published in March 2004 highlights this concern.

HOW CREDIT CARD HOLDERS REACT TO DISCLOSING INFORMATION ONLINE

More than 50 per cent of consumers recently surveyed by Jupiter Research Incorporated fear the personal information supplied in an online transaction will be sold to a retailer's marketing partners and generate unwanted marketing messages. More than a third of those surveyed also expressed concerns that unauthorised recurring transactions, such as subscription renewals, could result from supplying credit card information online. In the survey,

- 30 per cent of consumers worried about merchants not shipping products for which their credit card had been charged online;

- 20 per cent worried that a merchant could debit a card number supplied online for a higher price than the advertised price.

Older consumers were more concerned with identity theft – 63 per cent of those over age 55 surveyed saw it as a threat versus 56 per cent of those aged 18 to 24. Identity theft concerns lessened as consumers' online tenure increased. Among young and less-tenured consumers the greatest concern was merchant duplicity. For example, 32 per cent of those surveyed aged 18 to 24 expressed concern about being charged more than they agreed to pay at a checkout versus 20 per cent of survey respondents overall.

Confidence that technology solutions such as Verified by Visa could prevent fraud increased as online tenure increased. Significantly, Jupiter notes that 'newbies' (defined as those with only limited online tenure) will constitute a smaller portion of the overall online audience in years to come. As newbies will comprise a significantly lower percentage of the population moving forward it is necessary to present messages that focus increasingly on a tenured online population.

Food for thought, but bear in mind that this survey relates mainly to the North American market where online users are more attuned to purchasing by credit cards. A similar study for the UK where users are less attuned and even more cautious might paint a bleaker picture. Even so, you need to be tooled up to accept credit card payments and to assist you in selecting a system compatible with your requirements starting on the next page is a review of seven leading processors.

REVIEWING THE LEADING PAYMENT PROCESSORS

Website	PayPal (paypal.co.uk)
Setup/Monthly Fees	No/No
Orders By	Online Only
Locations	International with USA-bias
Processing Fees	Credit cards, 2.2% + 30 cents, no minimum Non-credit card, 1.6% + 30 cents
Extras	Payment to you is made into your bank account, or onto your credit card. Payments under $15 are only charged 30 cents.
Notes	Americans can use Web-Accept (accept credit card orders on their websites). International accounts can be opened, but are not able to use Web-Accept yet, although you can be paid by other PayPal users. Fee for $10 item 30 cents Fee for $100 item 250 cents Overall Cheapest Fees. A great service, cheaper than a merchant account.

Website	Verza Inc. (verza.com)
Setup/Monthly Fees	No/No
Orders By	Online Only
Locations	International
Processing Fees	Credit cards, 99 cents + 4.9%, Cheques, 99 cents + 3.5%.
Extras	Payments twice per month. 5% six-month rolling-reserve. Additional $15 for each chargeback. Includes an account control centre to view your account details and transaction logs.
Notes	Fee for $10 item 148 cents Fee for $100 item 589 cents

Website	Verotel (verotel.com)
Setup/Monthly Fees	No/No
Orders By	Cheques, credit cards and 1-900 number billing.
Locations	International
Processing Fees	Depends on transaction type and ticket price.
Extras	10% rolling reserve. $15 for each chargeback.
Notes	Credit card processing limited to **content**. Highly flexible service with several extras such as 'set up your own reseller programme free', 'real time control centre' and '1-900 billing'. Fee for $10 item 150 cents Fee for $75 (max by credit card) item 900 cents

Website	Internet Billing Company (ibill.com)
Setup/Monthly Fees	No/No
Orders By	Online
Locations	USA
Processing Fees	15% for up to $10,000 in sales per billing period. Graded reductions for increases in volume.
Extras	10% 6-month rolling reserve.
Notes	Limited to sales of access, content or services. Apparently, in order to use real time delivery with iBill, you need some custom CGI scripts. Fee for $10 item 150 cents Fee for $100 item 1500 cents

Website	**Shareit (shareit.com)**
Setup/Monthly Fees	No/No
Orders By	Online, Phone, Fax, Mail
Locations	USA + Germany
Processing Fees	$2.95 + 4%
Extras	Mailing a cheque = $5, issuing bank also deducts $5. Alternatively you can have payment wire transferred to your account. Cheques issued once per month.
Notes	They originally set out to act as a third party for shareware writers, but will accept credit card orders for any product or service. Based in Germany, are good for Europeans and allow you to accept the Euro as payment. Fee for $10 item 335 cents Fee for $100 item 695 cents

Website	**CC Now (ccnow.com)**
Setup/Monthly Fees	No/No
Orders By	Online
Locations	International
Processing Fees	9% (8% in Nov/Dec)
Extras	Reserve if your monthly volume is $1000+
Notes	Limited to sales of physical goods. Fee for $10 item 95 cents Fee for $100 item 950 cents

Website	Clickbank (clickbank.com)
Setup/Monthly Fees	$49.95/No
Orders By	Online
Locations	International
Processing Fees	$1.50 + 7.5%
Extras	No-longer free! Only issue cheques, and only if over $25. Charge $2.50 to process and send cheque. Withhold 10% of cheques over $25 which is released after approx 90 days. Cheques issued twice per month.
Notes	Service is limited to authors of unique internet content and services. If you distribute your own original information via web pages, files, or email, then ClickBank is ideal for you. You have the option to recruit resellers for your products, all details handled by Clickbank. You can also refer people to Clickbank and earn money if anyone you send to Clickbank signs up and makes sales. Not for sale of physical goods, recurring billing or with shopping carts. Fee for $10 item 225 cents Fee for $100 item 900 cents

OPTING FOR EITHER OF THE TWO MOST FAVOURED FACILITIES

Of these options I personally feel more comfortable using the first and last: Paypal and Clickbank. They are reliable, ultra security conscious, provide excellent account facilities, and always pay out on the due date.

MAJOR DRAWBACK AND HOW TO OVERCOME IT

ClickBank offers a magnificent service and I've always used it as my prime payment processor. It's fast, efficient, and above all, universally accepted. However, if you promote a multitude of digital products it has one much-heralded drawback. Either:

1. You are required to fork out another $49 every time you introduce a new creation on a disparate location, or ...

2. You are required to host all of your merchandise on one website.

Not any more; at least certainly not for me. You see, I have developed a safe, legitimate method of selling all of my ever-growing produce using ClickBank on a single fee of $49.

You can learn more about my secret system at this website:

howtoproducts-xl.com/ccc.html.

30
Giving stuff away for free to attract visitors

In Chapter 24 Shelley Lowery extolled the virtues of giving stuff away for free and just recently I decided to experiment myself in an endeavour to attract subscribers to my new newsletter.

I set up a website offering $370 worth of my own produce to every new subscriber.

Did my experiment work?

I'll let you judge for yourself ...

Within hours of submission of the URL this site rocketed to rank **No.15 out of 160,000,000** on Yahoo! (yes, one hundred and sixty million) competitive web pages with corresponding high rankings in all of the other major search engines.

Within hours the subscriptions started to pour in and (as I write) I have amassed over 3,000 in a matter of weeks ...

Category: Free Stuff > Web Directories
www.prospector.cz - 8k - Cached - More from this site - Save - Block

15. **Free Stuff For You** ≈
Free stuff for you; just one click and everything on this web page is yours for free! ... How-To FREE STUFF: One Click and It's All Yours! ... Just One click: All this free stuff is yours to download. ...
free-stuff-xl.com - 43k - Cached - More from this site - Save - Block

16. **Free** Center ≈
directory includes homepages, counters, graphics, fonts, and more.
Category: Shopping and Services > Free Stuff
www.freecenter.com - 34k - Cached - More from this site - Save - Block

17. **Free Stuff For You** ≈
Dedicated to linking fellow IBEW brothers and sisters and other union trade activists,
to provide information on labor issues and laws. ... Use this free space on the web to store your backup files, pictures, graphics, or whatever else you'd like. You can even ... JOIN the FREE STUFF email list today! ...
home.earthlink.net/~solidanty/free.html - 29k - Cached - More from this site - Save - Block

18. Top50 to ≈
features top list web directory, affiliate network, member community, website promotion, and more.
Category: Search Engines and Directories
www.top50.to - 68k - Cached - More from this site - Save - Block

19. No Junk **Free Stuff** ≈
updated and rated lists of free samples, e-mail accounts, and more.
Category: Shopping and Services > Free Stuff
www.nojunkfree.com - 23k - Cached - More from this site - Save - Block

TIP

I give my own stuff away for free but you don't have to ... just type 'free stuff' into the Google.com search engine and you will be presented with millions of cost-free opportunities.

31
Test marketing your online activities

Any good marketer knows that testing is the key to building profits in absolutely any business. You can never determine that one idea will or will not work in any specific business until you put it to the test. Don't think that the internet is any different.

- You have to test products.

- You have to test prices.

- You have to test promotional formats.

- You have to test headlines.

- You have to test ad copy.

- You have to test specific places to promote.

The testing process never ends. If you don't put your entire marketing plan to the test you will never truly know what can or cannot work. Every marketing test is an investment in your venture whether it produces results for you or not. It shows either a marketing method to keep working with or a method to avoid in your specific type of business. Take every single test you use as another lesson in your marketing education.

ARE YOU INVESTING OR GAMBLING IN YOUR ONLINE MARKETING?

The core problem in marketing presents itself when you start treating your advertising more like a gamble than an investment. Most internet businesses are just haphazardly wasting their money on every advertising opportunity that comes up. They don't key their ads and they don't take notes about what is working and why it is working. For some reason or other, the majority of marketers have developed an idea that the internet is somehow different from other promotional mediums. They think that if they just try enough different techniques, they may just magically come upon the technique that will make lots of money.

You can't just throw your money into promotion. You need to have a plan behind everything you do. You need to know when a technique is working so that you can run with it. You need to know what isn't working. Setting up the right testing mechanisms is the key to success in your marketing. You can't afford to gamble away whatever you earn from promotion.

HOW MUCH DOES YOUR WEBSITE MAKE PER VISITOR?

If you don't know the answer to this question then it isn't even possible for you to make informed decisions about what types of promotion you can use.

ESTABLISHING HOW MUCH TO SPEND ON WEBSITE VISITORS

If you don't know how much your website makes per visitor on average, how can you determine how much to spend to obtain each visitor? If your website brings in an average of a £1.00 per visitor, then you can afford to spend a lot more per visitor than a site which is bringing in only 5p per visitor. When you are using free advertising for your site you may not consider this to be very important, but once you start spending some of your cash flow on marketing, I can guarantee that if you don't know how much your site makes per visitor you are just working on a gamble.

COMPUTING YOUR INCOME AND UNIQUE VISITORS

The simplest method of determining your profit per visitor is to just add up your website income and all of your unique hits from the past month. Then divide the income by the number of visits you have received. That will give you a baseline number to get started with. As you start testing promotion more and more, you are also going to want to determine how many hits and how much profit you get from each type of ad. All visits are not created equal. Offline advertising will produce fewer visits than many types of online marketing, but usually they are of a much better quality than promotional formats such as banner ads. These offline visitors end up buying more stuff and having a much higher profit per visitor.

Your site could be making £2.00 per visitor from offline advertising and only 20p per visitor from banner ads. Getting those two types of visitors mixed up could cause you to make some very bad decisions about your advertising. That is where keying your ads and testing comes in. You must convert your promotion into a scientific investment instead of a haphazard gamble. You can do this most effectively by following a simple three-step system like the one I will show you below. It is the key to knowing which mediums are working for you – and which ones aren't.

INSTALLING A WEBSITE TRACKING SYSTEM

The first thing you will have to do to start finding out what type of advertising works for you is to set up some kind of tracking system. If you aren't tracking your visitors, then you can just forget about making intelligent marketing decisions. Also note that you need to be tracking more than just the overall traffic of your site. You need to know where people are going to on your site and you need each of your web pages tracked as well.

There are three simple ways to track your website stats:

1. You can use a free counter for each page on your website.

2. You can install a CGI program to track your stats.

3. You can purchase your domain where stats are part of the package.

MEASURING WEB PAGE EFFECTIVENESS WITH FREE COUNTERS

Superstats is the counter I use and recommend to you. The advantage of this method is that it is pretty simple to set up. You sign up for their service and then you insert their code into your site.

The disadvantage is that you will have a small link back to them on your site which may cost you a little traffic. An even bigger disadvantage is that you will need to sign up and insert a separate code on every one of your pages so that each page can be tracked separately. Having overall domain stats won't do you that much good if you don't know where they are coming from and who the buyers are.

v2.superstats.com/

INSTALLING CGI TO TRACK YOUR STATS

There are over 70 CGI programs out there which will track your stats for you. Make sure that you choose a program that tracks your stats on each page of your site. You don't want to have to use a separate CGI program for each page and you don't want all of your pages put together.

The advantage of using a CGI program is that you won't have to lose any traffic to outside sources and that some of the CGI programs can track all of your pages separately for you in one file. The disadvantage of this method is that it requires some programming knowledge and is often quite difficult to set up.

For a list of website counter programs, visit cgi.resourceindex.com/.

CHOOSING A HOSTING SERVICE WHERE STATS ARE PART OF THE DEAL

On my own current web hosts, stats for every single page of my sites are included. We talked about these particular hosting services in Chapter 11 but to refresh your memory, they are Third Sphere and Site Build It!

- Top pages are listed.

- Error messages that people receive are listed.

- Unique hits and page impressions for every single page are listed separately in these easy-to-use systems.

The essential advantage is that these are advanced tracking systems and simple to operate.

KEYING ALL YOUR PROMOTIONAL ACTIVITIES

You need to key all of your ads separately. The easiest way to do this is to make a copy of your sales letter on your site and create another site out of it. If your sales letter is named sales.htm, you could also make a sales1.htm, sales2.htm, sales3.htm, and so on. Then, use a different page as your website address for each ad you put out.

If you really want to track your advertising results effectively, you will also want to make copies of your order form. Then, you can know which ad is actually producing the sales and exactly how much money is coming in from every penny you spend. There are some other methods you could use to key your ads. For example, you could also set up an affiliate programme on your site and allocate each one a different affiliate number for each ad you place. This would automatically track all the sales for you. You could use different auto-responders for the responses. If you are doing a major offline advertising campaign, you could even set up a complete duplicate domain that you don't advertise any other way.

No matter which method you choose to use, the important thing is that you key and track every single one of your ads.

JUDGING RESULTS AND EXPANDING PROMOTION

After you have placed each ad, judge how it does. Did it produce a profit for you? If not, do you know why it didn't work? Try changing the headline, the body copy, or the advertising medium. Make only one of these changes at a time. If you change everything at once you will never know which aspect it was that created the change in results. If your ad did produce a profit, how can you expand on it? Try changing the headline or the ad slightly and see what the results are. Find other similar places that you could use to expand your advertising. Do this in a slow methodical way so you can track and keep increasing your profits with every ad you place.

If every ad you place is losing money then you are going to need to step back and re-examine your product, your market, your USP, and your overall concepts.

Are you selling what your market really wants and is it better than the competition?

Advertising never has to be a gamble. It can be an intelligent investment that will produce results for you time and time again. Look at the mutual fund manager. They may have 20 or more different stocks in their portfolio. While some of the stocks may lose money, the idea is to keep most of them making a profit.

- By combining all of the different stocks in one portfolio, they can reduce the risks and increase their chances of profit.

- By tracking all of your ads and using different forms of advertising, you can reduce your overall risk and then expand on whichever advertising pulls in the most profits.

Don't ever look at your marketing programme as a get rich quick scheme or you will end up gambling away your advertising budget.

Look at yourself as the mutual fund manager who intelligently picks and chooses the right sources for his or her portfolio.

Invest wisely.

TIP

You're thinking this is an almighty amount of work to be adding to your daily routine. It is. But if you do it, and do it consistently, you *will* make money online. You will also increase your awareness and enhance your marketing ...

32
How to analyse virtual footfall to improve your website

It pays to analyse the traffic to your virtual storefront or front office on a regular basis. If you use either of the hosting services recommended here (Third Sphere or Site Build It!) you will find that the required tracking tools are built into the system. If you use another service that doesn't provide this facility, then try this; type 'website statistics + free software' in to the Google search box and it will fetch up several options.

WHY IS IT IMPORTANT TO MONITOR YOUR VISITORS?

You get traffic to your website but what do they do when they reach your site?

- Do they visit the pages you want them to visit?

- Do they leave shortly after arriving?

- What pages are they interested in?

Armed with this important information you can tweak the content to help maximise virtual footfall interest. What good is it to have hundreds of visitors to your site if all they do is leave right away or look at pages that are not all that important to you?

THE STATISTICS REPORT CONTAINS ALL YOU NEED FOR ANALYSIS

Traffic

Page views: Page views are the number of times HTML pages are loaded in your visitor's browser. This indicates whether your website is interesting enough to look further into it and explore more pages.

Repeat visits: Determines who browsed your site more than once during the selected time period.

- Do you give your visitors a reason to return to your site?

- Is your site updated frequently with articles and content?

Activity

By time zone: Shows you what hour of the day they visited your site according to their time zone.

By local time: Shows you what hour of the day they visited your site according to your time zone.

Day of the week: Shows you the day of the week they visited; weekday or weekend. You can determine the best days to update your site or send out important information to your customers

Work/leisure time: What type of people visit your site can be determined from this information.

- Do people view your website during typical business hours or do they visit after they have gone home?

- Should you be concentrating on business people or what?

Navigation

Navigation paths: A navigation path is a sequence of pages that the visitor viewed from the moment they entered the site to the moment of departure. From the marketing viewpoint it is important to know the most common paths your visitors follow to get to the landing pages (that is the pages where the target events take place, such as ordering, file downloading, form filling and submission, etc.). You will learn which of the navigation paths are the most effective. The frequent exit patterns will show where your site is underperforming and you will see where to improve the content of your site to make your visitors' experience perfect.

Entry pages: The entry page that a visitor goes to when first visiting your website. By setting your links to go to specific pages of your website you can determine which referral links are working and which are not.

Exit pages: The exit page is where a visitor departs your site.

- Do your exit pages match your entry pages? If so, then see what you can do to fix your entry page to keep visitors on your site.
- Is it a navigation problem?
- Content not good enough?

Pages viewed after the home page: The success of your website depends on how short the journey from your home page to where your target page is. This also helps uncover navigation problems or lack of interest in your site.

Site stickiness: These are visits grouped by the time that visitors stay; it is a sign of how well a site's content captures the visitor's attention.

- Do they leave a few seconds after entering?
- Or are they thoroughly interested in what you have to say on your website?

Visitors

Unique visitors: This measures what a visitor does on the first visit only in a selected period of time. The software will grab specifically where they came from so you can tell the actions of one person visiting your site. In other words, if you have three unique visitors to your site ten times each instead of having a counter of 30 visitors you'll see three visitors and what pages they visited.

New visitors: This is a brand-new visitor, arriving at your site for the first time. New visitors are always unique, although they are not the same as 'unique visitors'. The number of new visitors will always be smaller than the number of unique visitors because a unique visitor is one arriving for the first time in the selected period (so the system may identify the visitor as unique in the current period but it also knows that they have been before). A new visitor is one on his first visit. This will tell you if your website is attracting new customers.

Frequent visitors: This report tells you how many times a certain visitor visits your site.

- Do they only visit your website once?

- A few times a day?

- Once a week?

- Several times a week?

This analysis is important to find out if people view your site as something to come back to and it lets you know if you need to make changes to keep people coming back.

Motivated visitors: If two or more pages are browsed during a visit, this will be counted in the Motivated Visits report. The ratio of visits when more than one page is viewed to all visits is a good sign of your site's attractiveness.

New visitors' second visits: This report lets you know how many of the new visitors returned to your site. Not to be confused with repeat visitors because this one monitors only the new ones.

Visit frequency: The number of return visits undertaken by all of your visitors.

- Does the highest percentage of your visitors visit only once?
- 2–4 visits?
- 5–10 visits?
- Or as many as 300 visits?

Referrers

The reports here show you where your visitors came from.

Bookmarked pages: Do people bookmark your website to visit later?

Search engines: What search engine did they use?

- What keyword did they type in?
- Which keywords are the most popular?

Adjust your website to the popular keywords.

Referring pages (links): What other websites did your visitors come from? Concentrate on the higher traffic links.

Pages

Popular pages: What area of the site are people most interested in?

Unpopular pages: Are these pages to fix or delete?

Views per visit: How many pages are viewed during the visit?

Views per first visit: How many pages do first time visitors view?

Page stickiness: How long do they stay on different pages? Should you fix or delete the pages people don't spend much time on?

Systems

Browsers and browser versions: It is a good idea to see what the majority of your visitors view your website in. What does your site look like in their browser? Try it; you may be surprised to find out that some content is not readable or supported. Or it may make your site look awful.

Operating systems: Are your visitors using Windows, Macintosh, Linux, or WebTV?

Windows versions: Are your visitors up-to-date or are they still using Windows 95?

Screen resolutions: What screen resolution do people view your site on? If a substantial number use 800 x 600 pixels do they have to scroll right and left to read the content?

Colour palettes: What capability do your visitors' computers have? Should you concentrate more on using 'web safe colours' in your design?

Cookie and Java Support: Do you use these scripts on your website? If your visitors have these turned off, they may not be able to view important sections of your site. If a substantial number of people have this support turned off consider using other options.

Demographics

Countries: What countries are your visitors from? Does this pose a problem?

Languages: What language do they use? If you see a growing number of a foreign language, consider making your site bilingual.

Time zones: What time zone are they coming from?

33
Servicing your customers online

You might just get away for a time with marketing a substandard product but as you well know as a responsible small business person, you'll never get away at any time with providing inferior service. You'll be found out in a hundred different ways. In the bricks and mortar environment the essential elements in the provision of good service tend to vary from one industry to another, but they are all directed towards the one end: **keeping the customer happy**. No one lasts long in retailing, for example, unless time and energy are constantly expended on matters such as enhancing store lighting, improving ease of traffic flow, extending the range of options to pay, and excelling in customer care.

WHY THE INTERNET PRESENTS AN AVENUE OF OPPORTUNITY

The pressure is unrelenting and the demands increase in tandem with the changes in trading patterns occasioned by the phenomenal growth of information technology. And yet in this very technology lies an avenue of opportunity if we but take the time to examine it. Most small businesses nowadays have an internet presence of sorts in the shape of a modestly constructed website. But how many of them use it for the purpose the web was invented: the receipt *and* distribution of valuable information?

Your website provides a powerful way to foster good customer relations and to engender loyalty by providing a constant stream of information on all matters relating to service.

IT'S CALLED 'E-SERVICE'

Here's how it works and you can tailor it to your own particular requirements.

8 SECRETS FOR SUCCESSFUL E-SERVICE

Effective e-service, despite the apparent obstacles, is actually a very achievable goal. As numerous successful implementers have demonstrated, it simply requires the right principles, practices, and tools. Eight basic attributes make web-based customer support work for any business, no matter how small:

1. **Making sure your website 'listens' to customers** – Every successful salesperson knows the most important part of their job is listening – both for explicit and implicit messages. websites should do the same. Explicit messages are clear requests for specific information. Implicit messages are patterns of queries or usage that imply a lack of, or difficulty in, finding some type of content. An effective web presence requires mechanisms and/or practices that ensure an attentive ear to both types of online customer requirements.

2. **Giving customers what they want** – It's not enough to ascertain which types of content users are asking for: the content must also be provided quickly. The atmosphere of the web is driven by a sense of immediacy. Delays in delivering customer-driven content can be deadly. An e-service solution must capture customer requests and use that information to automatically enhance site content for future visitors.

3. **Responsive content and response mechanisms that are easy to find and easy to use** – It's remarkable how many website designers allow customers to wind up in places where they can't easily find a way to ask for more information or send an email request. On many sites, the 'Contact Us' button simply launches a pre-addressed email screen – with no information about how

soon they can expect a reply or where else to look for information. Many sites don't even provide a phone number if a customer really needs to talk to someone right away. If customers can't even find the company phone number, what are the chances that they will be able to find an even more obscure piece of information? *Hidden content is the same as no content at all.* Of course, this is true of all types of content, but it's especially critical for response-related pages. So e-service must be easy for customers to use.

4. **Appreciating the 80/20 rule** – While it's great to make sure website content is as comprehensive as possible, the fact remains that – on average – *80% of all site traffic is aimed at 20% of the content.* In other words, a relatively small amount of content can take care of a tremendous amount of business if it's the right content. So small businesses that delay putting up sites because they're trying to make sure they can answer every possible customer question online are making a mistake. It's much smarter to get the most important information up first, and then add to it over time as dictated by customer needs.

5. **Why it pays to get pushy** – You don't have to rely on customers coming to your site to get them the information they need. *By offering a variety of email notification options, you can turn a customer's email box into an extension of your website.* A good way to do this is to ask visitors if they would like to be notified if there is any change in a specified content area, such as a product catalogue or a press release archive. Such notify-on-change 'push' mechanisms allow you to promote your website and build an ongoing electronic relationship with your customers.

6. **Respond quickly or risk losing the customer forever** – As highlighted in a recent major study based on consumer feedback (*Right Now Technology Study, 2005*) many businesses make the mistake of being too slow in their response to online information requests. Once a customer or prospect has been disappointed by how slowly their question has been answered, they are unlikely

to try again. They might even become disillusioned about the operation as a whole. If you're going to offer even a bare bones email contact mechanism, make sure it results in a fast reply – preferably as early as possible on the following working day.

7. **Track for information as it comes in** – Because a large percentage of site visitors tend to have the same narrow set of questions, it's critically important to track requests for information as they come in. Consistent tracking of requests allows those in charge of site content to determine where to direct their efforts – allowing for much more efficient use of resources. Effective e-service applications perform this tracking automatically and dynamically rank information based on historical usefulness to customers. This 'sameness' in questions is all the more reason to include a FAQ (frequently asked questions) section on the website.

8. **Automate, automate, automate** – All the tasks required to create a truly responsive site – assimilating and analysing user queries, developing appropriate content and posting it in a well-organised manner, handling *ad hoc* and 'push' email communications, etc. – can be extremely labour-intensive. As site traffic increases, these tasks can pile up even more. *Many sites are spoiled by their own success, as the volume of communications exceeds the resources dedicated to supporting that communication.* So, it is critically important to deploy effective automation tools that can be modified to meet rising demands. Such tools significantly increase the return on staff and infrastructure resources invested in the web. Good e-service applications automate site maintenance tasks and eliminate time-consuming knowledge collection and engineering functions – functions that, when neglected over time, result in out-of-date content and dissatisfied customers.

These simple procedures can make the difference between online success and online failure. As so many operations continue to demonstrate, online success not only has an impact on how a company is perceived by its customers, but also on how it is perceived by internet users *en masse*.

Visit www.rightnowtechnologies.com for a comprehensive review on all matters relating to the successful implementation of your own e-service facility.

WHY IT PAYS TO SURVEY YOUR WEBSITE VISITORS

A good way to kick off your e-service project is to set up a simple 'feedback' form. Asking for feedback from visitors to your site is one of the best ways to obtain suggestions about improving your merchandise—and an online survey is a fast, convenient and inexpensive method to gather information, including:

1. What do your customers and prospects want to buy?

2. How do they like your current product or service?

3. How would they improve it?

4. What do they think of your competition?

Always respond quickly with a 'thank you' email for their participation. This helps create a bond that keeps customers and converts prospects.

34
What online marketing cannot do for you

While there's no question that a solid online marketing programme can increase your business, there are certain things it cannot do.

MARKETING CAN'T MAKE YOU AN OVERNIGHT SUCCESS

Just because you engage in online marketing doesn't mean you are immediately going to see your business explode. Marketing is about getting your name in front of your target market on a regular basis until they finally decide to give you a try.

On that note, if you're in trouble right now: sales are down, a new business isn't getting off the ground as you'd planned; then depending on how serious the trouble is, online marketing may not be enough to save you. Any successful marketing strategy needs time to work and more often than not, a little money as well. If you're panicked about one or both, you may need to start looking at other options.

MARKETING IS NOT ABOUT DOING SOMETHING ONCE AND FORGETTING ABOUT IT

The very best marketers test. And test. And test again.

For instance, maybe your website isn't converting visitors to customers as well as it should be.

- You could hire a copywriter to tweak it for you.

- You could test the different elements to see what raises your conversion level.

- You could test different headlines, different offers, etc.

MARKETING CAN'T FIX A BAD EXPERIENCE

This is a big one. If your customers have a bad experience with your products or services or with your customer service or sales support, that's it. Worse yet, not only have you lost a customer for good, that customer will probably tell others about their bad experience.

So now you've lost potential customers as well.

Marketing can get people in the door but it cannot ensure they will have an experience they'd want to repeat. So before assuming more marketing is what you need, take a moment and make sure your current customers are truly satisfied with your business.

MARKETING CAN'T REPAIR A FLAWED BUSINESS

Marketing can't fix cash flow issues or staff problems.

Sometimes you get so caught up in the day-to-day challenges of running a business you can't see the woods for the trees.

Suppose you have a business that's struggling with cash flow. The first thing that springs to mind may be revving up marketing. After all, the idea behind marketing is to increase revenue. On the surface that makes good sense. However, if you look a little closer, what you might find are expenses that are out of whack, or you are not getting your invoices out in a timely manner. So what you should be fixing is accounting problems rather than changing your marketing.

MARKETING CAN'T MAKE PEOPLE BUY THINGS THEY DON'T WANT OR CAN'T AFFORD

It doesn't matter how great your product or service is, if you're selling to people who either don't have the interest or the means to buy it, then your marketing is going to fail no matter how brilliant it may be.

So basically it all boils down to this, before you decide you need more marketing, take a few moments and make sure that online marketing is really the right solution for your business.

CREATIVITY EXERCISE – REALITY CHECK

Before you launch into online marketing, take some time to analyse what's really happening in your business. Do you really need a marketing program or is your problem connected with any of these factors:

- You aren't able to close the leads you have.

- You aren't invoicing in a timely manner or following up with unpaid accounts.

- Your customers aren't happy with the product or service.

- Your customers are having a bad experience with technical support or something else in the process isn't working.

- Your target market isn't right.

- You aren't passionate about what you're doing any more.

- Your business is over-expensed.

If you want to grow your business, then you should be *consistently* marketing your business, but if you're using marketing as a band-aid for some other problem, then you could be heading for trouble.

I am indebted to a fellow writer Michele Pariza Wacek for the wisdom contained in this brief chapter. Michele is the author of *Got Ideas? Unleash Your Creativity and Make More Money.*

www.TheArtistSoul.com

35
Channeling your online fame into offline activity

As your online fame grows it opens the doors to opportunities offline; opportunities to enhance your reputation and create strings of incremental income.

GUESTING AT SEMINARS

You will be invited (as I frequently am) to feature as a speaker in both offline and online seminars – and it won't be your accent they're interested in – but your expert knowledge; the expertise you demonstrate in your articles, your books, your web copy, your marketing.

Don't be bashful when opportunity knocks.

Agree to participate, cash in on your growing fame, and you will in the process sell more of your merchandise, passively and automatically.

GUESTING IN BROADCAST MEDIA

As your status as an expert in your chosen field of activity spreads, you may well receive invitations to appear as a guest on appropriate local radio and television programmes. I can best illustrate the power of such live appearances by reproducing one of my articles. It appears in all the major ezine hubs and still brings thousands of visitors to my websites ...

Can You Really Sell Your Writing Output On Radio?

by Jim Green

I had never given the matter much thought in the past but after an experience I enjoyed lately, I am now rather of the opinion that you can.

It happened this way …

Coinciding with the launch of my latest book 'Your Retirement Masterplan' (How To Books ISBN 1857039874) I participated in eleven 10/15 minute live interviews on local radio over a period of just five days.

These promotional interviews were arranged by my publisher's media consultancy and I didn't need to visit a single studio to take part; they were all conducted over the telephone, sitting at my desk at home.

Towards the end of the first interview I was conscious of the fact that I had yet to plug the distribution channels for my book.

The presenter beat me to it: 'In five seconds, where can listeners buy your book?' Before I could reply he added, 'Can they order it online?'

'Yes,' I said, 'at Amazon.co.uk'.

In the ten subsequent interviews I made a point of ending my spiel with the publisher's name together with availability at bookstores but I always finished with, ' …and online at Amazon.co.uk.'

Now here's the interesting part: after the first five sessions I checked out the Amazon.co.uk website to discover that this newly published title had jumped 35 places in the bestseller list for its genre; I checked again after the final interview and it had jumped again but this time by 329 places. In effect, in just a few days it had leapt from position 558 to 194 out of 3,123 competing titles.

More than mere coincidence methinks … because books don't climb the bestseller lists on Amazon unless they are selling in quantity.

So what if you self-publish your output and you don't have a publicist to arrange radio interviews? Does that mean you are excluded?

No way; I have self-published several books in the past and managed my own promotion.

Here is what you do …

1. Wherever you live in the world you'll find that the majority of local radio stations are banded together into a single group for cost-effectiveness;

2. Identify the controlling group;

3. Visit the corporate website containing links to all subsidiaries;

4. Pick out those stations within a 500/1,000 mile orbit;

5. Visit each local station website individually;

6. Scan the daily programming schedules;

7. Highlight those shows that might identify with the topic of your book;

8. Note the presenter's name;

9. Email him/her with a well-couched request for a live interview;

10. Follow that up with an identical snail mail request;

11. Follow that up with a telephone call (you'll get to speak to someone in authority);

12. You know your topic inside out; speak up with confidence and you'll get your interview; maybe not straightaway but, if you sell yourself and your project professionally, you'll be logged into an up-and-coming slot in the station scheduling.

Go for it …it's free!

Postscript: Those eleven live interviews did more than sell books on radio – they resulted in several direct invitations to repeat my pitch on local television.

Milking incremental income streams as an author

As your book(s) become available online and offline your reputation as an expert in your particular subject will flourish. This brings with it additional opportunities for attracting incremental income; opportunities such as ...

1. Public speaking engagements;

2. Book reviewing;

3. Magazine article contributions;

4. Foreign translations of your work;

5. Book club sales;

6. Public Lending Right (PLR); you get paid every time someone borrows your book from a public lending library;

7. Fees under license (when another publisher reproduces your work);

8. Broadcasting rights;

9. Audio tape and disc rights.

The fees you earn are incremental to your book royalties and they soon mount up over a period of time. My new creative writing course 'Secrets to Churning Out Bestsellers' contains several chapters on how to milk these additional income streams. http://www.1st-creative-writing-course.com

About the author

Jim Green is a bestselling author with an ever-growing string of niche non-fiction titles to his credit. 'Secrets to Churning Out Bestsellers' is his latest dynamic creative writing course and is available for immediate download at

www.1st-creative-writing-course.com and www.writing-for-profit.com.

TIP

In whichever direction your online fame takes off, always be on the lookout for opportunities to enhance your reputation offline at zero cost.

36
Getting it all together to grow your small business rapidly

We have reached the end of our journey on the formation of a plan to grow your small business rapidly online. In a nutshell: **It's all about joined-up marketing**; how everything you do is joined together. There are no random events; none whatever. One act leads to another in the logical progression for success and *if you don't understand this one simple, but vital point* your enterprise will stutter and stumble until it grinds to a halt.

DEVISING AN ONLINE MARKETING VEHICLE; NOT JUST A WEBSITE

- What is the purpose for which the internet was devised?

- Could you use that purpose to your advantage?

- How would you go about doing that?

- What is the value of a good website to the small business owner?

- How would you keep pace with the opportunities offered by the internet?

- What two things do you need to make online marketing work for you?

(Pages 1 to 9)

LEARNING HOW EVEN THE SMALLEST ENTERPRISE CAN PROSPER ONLINE

- How can online activity offset adverse conditions offline?
- Will you bin negative thinking in your approach to online marketing?
- Will you set yourself a challenge for online success?
- Will you pull out all the stops to achieve it?

(Pages 10 to 15)

WHY ONLINE MARKETING IS TAILOR-MADE FOR SMALL BUSINESS

- How many good reasons are there for growing your business online?
- How many of these can you remember?
- Why do you still need a website when you do all your business offline?
- Why is the internet such a dynamic marketing tool?

(Pages 16 to 20)

CONVERTING YOUR LOCAL BUSINESS INTO AN INTERNATIONAL CONCERN

- How can you benefit from the global dual knock-on effect?
- How do you determine whether you qualify?
- How would you evaluate your intellectual properties for online application?
- How would you confirm what you *think* you know?
- How would you go about adding to your knowledge?

- How would you convert your intellectual properties into digital products?

- How would you promote them?

- What do you know about accepting credit card payments online?

(Pages 23 to 27)

HOW TO BECOME ACKNOWLEDGED AS AN EXPERT IN YOUR NICHE

- Where is it easier to be accepted as an expert: online or offline?

- What does the power of recognition as an expert in your niche mean for you?

- What tools will you need to mark your expertise?

- How will you use them?

- Why is providing solutions to problems so important online?

(Pages 28 to 32)

HOW TO MAKE YOUR PRODUCE OR SERVICE FAMOUS ONLINE

- How does online fame promote your produce?

- How does its 'secrecy' keep you secure?

- How would you capitalise on the amazing power of your own name?

- How do articles increase your online fame?

- How do you swamp the Web with your own articles?

- How do you turn your articles into top grade press releases?

- How does linking to other websites increase your fame?

- What does the term 'electronic spiders' refer to?
- How do they help generate top ten rankings on demand?
- Could you produce your own online newspaper – and why?
- Could you get prospects queuing up in droves to subscribe?
- Why does it pay to give stuff away for free online?
- Could you convert online fame into offline activity?
- What is the hidden power behind becoming famous online?

(Pages 33 to 38)

DEVISING THE PLAN FOR MARKETING YOUR ENTERPRISE ONLINE

- What must you think about seriously first before starting on your plan?
- Why is it dangerous to chop and change your strategy?
- Which questions should you be asking yourself?
- What will you mission statement contain?
- Will you be staying local or going global?
- How will you decide what to include in your website?
- What will be your domain name?
- Will you plan to promote your website both online and offline?
- What allowance will you be making for start-up costs?
- Will you budget time for servicing the website?
- How will you legislate to deliver superior customer service online?
- What will you do to foster loyalty among your existing offline clientele?

- What plans do you have to monitor the competition online?

- Will you source for merchandise and suppliers online?

- Will you be tracking market trends online?

- Will you be providing an online ordering service for customers?

- Will you be setting up your own online newsletter?

- What else should you be including in your plan?

(Pages 40 to 45)

WHY MARKETING ON THE INTERNET IS FAST, EASY AND STRESS-FREE

- Can you name the ten inbuilt advantages to marketing a small business online?

- How does online marketing facilitate cutting start-up costs to the bone?

- How is it you can choose your own hours for online marketing?

- How come there is round the clock order-taking online?

- How does your local virtual store manage to reach out internationally?

- Why is it you will be managing your online affairs on a level playing field?

- What are the choices open to potential online customers?

- How do virtual transactions get the cash in fast?

- Why is it win-win all round online?

- How does customer satisfaction result in additional sales?

- Why does virtual customer interfacing cut down on stress?

(Pages 46 to 57)

WHY NICHE MARKETING WORKS BEST FOR SMALL BUSINESS

- What must you do before you start looking for a niche?

- Why is it impractical to try selling everything to everyone?

- How can you risk failure before you even start?

- What outstrips all other e-commerce niche purchasing options?

- Do people buy what they need – or what they want?

- How does niche nous sustain success?

- How can you spot an easy-to-target niche market?

- Why is it important to develop products and services that provide solutions?

- How do you test the potential for your niche market?

(Pages 52 to 58)

HOW TO DEVISE A DOMAIN NAME THAT REFLECTS YOUR ENTERPRISE

- What is the catalyst that drives the engine online?

- Why is it vital to apply fitness to purpose in choosing a domain name?

- What are the essential do's-and-don'ts in domain name selection?

(Pages 61 to 64)

CREATING A WEBSITE TO YOUR EXACT REQUIREMENTS

- What is the difference between mini- and maxi-websites?

- Which of these is the perfect vehicle for small business?

- What are online sales letters styled in the advertorial format?

- Why do these work well for small business?

- What are the components of the ideal virtual sales letter?

- What is the all-in-one solution for devising mini-sites?

- What is the perfect web hosting service for mini-sites?

- In what circumstances would you need to adopt the multi-page approach?

- What is the cutting-edge tool that does it all automatically?

- How would you go about creating and managing a multi-page website?

(Pages 68 to 73)

CONSTRUCTING CONTENT-RICH PAGES TO SNARE THE SPIDERS

- Why are you already an experienced writer but you don't credit yourself?

- What are the offline writing techniques that work equally well online?

- What are the vital factors pointing the way to good web writing?

- How do you encourage interaction with your website visitors?

- How can you lace your text with keywords to entice the spiders?

(Pages 75 to 85)

WRITING SALES COPY THAT SIZZLES

- What are the guidelines for producing sizzling sales letters?

- What can market traders teach you about good presentation?

- Which concept can you use to develop dozens of online products?

(Pages 86 to 89)

THE INCREDIBLE POWER OF KEYWORDS

- What happens to website footfall when you target the right keywords?

- What do people do when they do a search online?

- Why it pays to think as your customers would.

- Why does homing in on niche keywords produce instant results?

- How does keyword power impact on sales?

- Where can you find free software to assist in detecting power keywords?

(Pages 92 to 96)

AVOIDING SEARCH ENGINE POSITIONING ERRORS

- Why should you never optimise your website with inappropriate keywords?

- What happens when you overload the Meta tag with keywords?

- What happens when you use the same keywords over and over again?

- Why is using the hidden text technique a no-no?

- And similarly, pages with an over-abundance of graphics and marginal text?

- Why do search engines reject keyword-rich text in the 'no frames' tag?

- And similarly, the use of page cloaking?

- Why is over-reliance on automatic submission tools unacceptable?

- And similarly, over-submitting pages on a daily basis?

- Why is it pointless to over-concentrate on search engine submission?

(Pages 97 to 101)

SNARING THE SPIDERS TO GENERATE TOP RANKINGS ON DEMAND

- Follow this tried and tested technique and you will hit the high spots.

- How to overcome search engine paralysis.

(Pages 103 to 110)

HOW TO USE SITE MAPS TO INCREASE TRAFFIC FLOW

- Should a site map be spider food or just a light snack?

- Do you know how to give the spiders a tasty treat?

- Does every site need a site map?

(Pages 114 to 116)

FLOODING YOUR SITE WITH LOW- AND NO-COST TRAFFIC

- Why does it pay to invest in the pay-per-click search engines?

- And similarly, participation in newsgroups, forums, mailing lists?

- Why do small business operators exchange links with other websites?

- Why does creating articles for newsletters and magazines produce dividends?

- How do you trigger interest with free press releases?

(Pages 117 to 120)

HOW TO CONVERT YOUR EXPERTISE INTO DIGITAL PRODUCE

- How do you create virtual book covers automatically?

- Why is it important to have a cover for your information product?

- Could you create a strategy for sales and distribution?

- Why will it pay you to give some of your ebooks away for free?

- Do you know you can create your own software programs?

(Pages 122 to 126)

HOW THE AMAZING AUTHORITY OF ARTICLES ATTRACTS VISITORS

- Why do successful e-entrepreneurs use articles to attract visitors?

- Do you know what to do before you start writing your own articles?

- What's the worst thing that can happen with every article you publish?

- Do you know where to submit your article output?

- Which article hubs distribute your material for free?

- Which software does it all automatically?

- Could you convert your articles into press releases?

- How do you drive hoards of traffic to your website?

- Which technique produces staggering results?

(Pages 127 to 140)

THE POWER OF LINKING TO OTHER WEBSITES

- What are the easy zero-cost steps for building link popularity?

- How does your site get those coveted inbound links?

- How do you prepare your site before you start looking for links?

- Would you budget time for link building?

- Would you establish realistic linking goals?

- Would you be selective about the sites from which you request links?

- Would you develop a relationship with linking sites?

- Would you provide linking codes?

- Would you strive to attain directory listings?

- Would you consider bartering for links?

(Pages 141 to 149)

UNDERSTANDING THE CHANGING FACE OF EMAIL MARKETING

- What is the controversy surrounding bulk email?

- Is there a better, more legitimate way than bulk mailing?

- What are the basic excuses for not implementing opt-in email?

- What are the common email mistakes you must avoid at all costs?

- What 12 careless practices sabotage email marketing?

- How can you earn more using email efficiently?

- Why does email make everything easier and faster?

(Pages 150 to 160)

WHY YOU MUST CREATE YOUR OWN NEWSLETTER

- What are the goals all newsletter publishers strive to achieve?
- What are the incentives in submitting your newsletter to directories?
- What are the secrets that convert your newsletter into a cash machine?

(Pages 161 to 165)

HOW BUILDING LISTS ATTRACTS SALES

- What are the secrets to building massive opt-in lists?
- Would you use incentives to obtain subscribers?
- Would you use pop-up windows?
- What is the value of alert boxes?

(Pages 168 to 170)

WHY YOU SHOULD CONSIDER ADDING 'BLOGGING' TO YOUR MARKETING

- What exactly is blogging?
- Would publishing your private thoughts unnerve you?
- Do blogs provide feedback?
- Can you post images on blogs?
- Can you send blogs using your mobile?
- How would you get started on blogging?

(Pages 173 to 176)

HOW RSS CAN GALVANISE EXPOSURE

- What is RSS?

- How does it provide a new, untapped marketing channel?

- Can it eliminate the spam filter nuisance?

- Does it sound to you too good to be true?

- Why have most online marketers never heard of RSS?

- What can RSS do for your small business online marketing?

(Pages 177 to 178)

IT MAKES SENSE TO ALLOW GOOGLE TO ADD TO YOUR INCOME

- What is Adsense?

- Can you make money from it?

- Can Adsense be targeted to your website content?

- Does it cost to join Adsense?

- Does it allow you to place a Google search box on your site?

- How would you benefit from that?

- Can you customise the appearance of the ads?

- Can you run Adsense on all or just selected pages?

(Pages 180 to 183)

TURNING PROSPECTS INTO CASH-PAYING CUSTOMERS

- What mistakes stop people buying from you?

- What is the golden rule of selling online?

(Pages 184 to 186)

SETTING UP YOUR OWN ONLINE PAYMENT SYSTEM

- How do credit card holders react to disclosing information online?
- Can you name two of the leading payment processors?
- Why are these the most favoured options?
- What is the major drawback with ClickBank?
- How would you overcome it?

(Pages 188 to 193)

HOW GIVING STUFF AWAY FOR FREE ATTRACTS VISITORS

- Did you read about my experiment?
- How did it pan out in practice?

(Pages 195 to 196)

WHY YOU MUST TEST MARKET EVERYTHING YOU DO

- Are you investing or gambling in your online marketing?
- How much does your website make per visitor?
- How do you establish how much to spend on website visitors?
- How do you compute your income and unique visitors?
- How would you install a website tracking system?
- How do you measure web page effectiveness?
- Would you install CGI to track your stats?
- How do you choose a hosting service where stats are part of the deal?
- How do you key all your promotional activities?

(Pages 197 to 202)

HOW TO ANALYSE YOUR VIRTUAL FOOTFALL

- Why is it important to monitor your visitors?

- Which report contains all you need for analysis?

(Pages 204 to 205)

HOW TO SERVICE CUSTOMERS ONLINE

- How does the internet present an opportunity for customer service?

- Describe 'e-service'.

- What are the eight secrets for successful e-service?

- Why does it pay to survey your website visitors?

(Pages 210 to 214)

WHY ONLINE MARKETING ISN'T A PANACEA FOR EVERY ILL

- Would you expect overnight results from your marketing?

- Why isn't marketing something you only do once?

- Can marketing fix a bad experience with a customer?

- Can marketing repair a flawed business?

- Can marketing persuade people to buy things they don't want or can't afford?

- Have you tried a reality check on your own small business?

(Pages 215 to 217)

CHANNELING YOUR ONLINE FAME INTO OFFLINE ACTIVITY

- Could you be a guest at seminars?

- Could you obtain invitations to appear in broadcast media?

(Pages 219 to 222)

FINAL WORDS

Now you have the first of the two things that are essential to the small business owner who wishes to become successful in online marketing: *the knowledge*.

The *application* is all up to you now ...

Good luck.

Glossary

Alert box

Mini-window that pops up or slides onto a web page to make an announcement.

Automatic payment processing

Electronic system; completes transactions from secure server and fulfils orders automatically.

Blog

Website where you write on an ongoing basis; a personal diary; a daily pulpit; a collaborative space; a political soapbox; a breaking-news outlet; a collection of links ...

Bulk email

Practice of sending email in bulk without permission of the recipients; frowned upon by the internet authorities.

Content-rich webpage

Web page copy interlaced with keywords to attract the search engine spiders.

Digital produce

Produce such as informational merchandise and software that is digitised and marketed online.

Directory listing

Having a website catalogued in the major online registers such as Google, Yahoo!, etc.

Discussion board

Electronic noticeboard where visitors can post messages and items of interest to other online users.

Domain name

The URL (uniform resource locator) or address for a website.

Ebook

Transcript that is manufactured in digital format; such as book, document, article, etc.

E-commerce

The practice of buying and selling online.

Email marketing

Promoting merchandise online using email as the vehicle for relaying sales messages to prospective buyers.

E-service

Practice of servicing customers' requirements online.

EXE

(Short for Executable Extension and pronounced *ee-ex-ee*) is an executable file with a .exe extension.

Ezine

An electronic newsletter.

FFA sites

Websites which operate a free-for-all service in accepting advertising material.

FTP

(File Transfer Protocol) system for uploading files from one website to another.

Google.com

The leading online search engine.

Google AdSense

Programme that generates advertising revenue with no financial outlay, minimal investment in time, and no additional resources.

Graphics library
Facility within a website or hosting service for storing digital images.

Information product
Generally ascribed to informational produce that has been digitally manufactured for resale or to be given away online.

Intellectual property
Something that has been conceived and developed in the mind.

Joint venture
Practice of entering into an agreement with another online user to resell goods or services.

Keyword
Core word that is included in web page text as an aid to defining overall context.

Keyword phrase
Key words paired together to achieve same result.

Link popularity
The extent, as measured by the quality of its text links to other websites, to which a website is favoured by search engines and users alike.

Links and banners
Text links and image banners which interact electronically with other websites.

List building
The process of building a list of prospective customers or parties interested in an online marketing proposition.

Maxi-website
Website consisting of multiple pages.

Mini-website
Website consisting of 1, 2 or 3 pages only.

Multi-dimensional website
A website consisting of multiple pages of diverse data.

Multiple income streams
The process of developing a string of online money-making opportunities.

Niche
Tiny but popular markets, produce, customer classifications.

Offline
Any business that conducts its affairs without using the internet.

One-page website
A website consisting of a single page.

Online footfall
Website traffic.

Online forum
An online meeting place for like-minded enthusiasts on a given topic.

Online research
Research undertaken using internet facilities.

Online survey
Market or consumer survey conducted on the internet.

Page cloaking
Page cloaking is a technique used to deliver different web pages under different circumstances. People generally use page cloaking for two reasons: (1) to hide the source code of their search engine optimised pages from their competitors and (2) to prevent human visitors from having to see a page which looks good to the search engines but does not necessarily look good to them.

Password protected page
Web page that requires a password before permission is granted to enter.

Pay-per-click
The process whereby internet users pay a fee to attract visitors to their websites.

PDF
(Portable Document Folder) captures formatting information from a variety of desktop publishing applications; can be read on any computer anywhere in the world.

RSS
Family of XML file formats for web syndication used by news websites and weblogs.

Search engine positioning
Search engine optimised web pages that drive targeted traffic to websites; also known as Gateway or Doorway pages.

Search engine spiders
Electronic robots that travel through the internet assessing website suitability for inclusion in search engine listings.

Secure space
The provision of web space to house sensitive data within a site.

Site map
Digital map that facilitates visits to every page on a website.

Spam blockers
Software to obstruct uninvited email messages arriving in a user's inbox.

Spiders
Term applied to electronic robots that visit websites to assess value for search engine positioning.

Test marketing
The practice of testing out the potential of a product or service before launching it in the marketplace.

Useful reading

Electronic Marketing for Small Business: Low-Cost/High Return Tools and Techniques that Really Work, Tom Antion (John Wiley & Sons 2005)

The E-Code, Joe Vitale & Jo Han Mok, (John Wiley 2005)

Low-Budget Online Marketing, Holly Berkeley, (Self Counsel Press 2005)

43 Ways to Make Money Online, Joe Vitale and Jo Han Mock, (John Wiley & Sons 2005)

Small Business Marketing for Dummies, Barbara Findlay Schenk, (Hungry Minds Inc, U.S. 2nd edition 2005)

Success with Online Retailing for Small Business, Patrick Tan, (iUniverse.com, US 2003)

Developing Your Online Business Profitability, Martin Brighty & Dean Markham, (Spiro Press 2003)

Little E, Big Commerce: How to Make a Profit Online, Sir Richard Branson (Foreword), Timothy Cumming, (Virgin Books 2001)

Starting an Online Business for Dummies, Greg Holden, (Hungry Minds Inc 2002)

Small Business Websites That Work, Sean McManus, (Prentice Hall 2003)

The Complete Idiot's Guide to Starting a Business Online, Frank Fiore, (Que 2000)

The Online Copywriter's Handbook: Everything You Need to Know to Write Electronic Copy That Sells, Robert W. Bly, (Contemporary Books 2003)

Multiple Streams of Internet Income: How Ordinary People Make Extraordinary Money Online, Robert Allen, (John Wiley & Sons Inc 2002)

New Ideas About New Ideas: Insights on Creativity from the World's Leading Innovators, Shira P. White & G.Patton Wright, (Financial Times Prentice Hall 2002)

Why They Don't Buy: Make Your Online Customer Experience Work, Max Mckeown, (Financial Times Prentice Hall 2001)

Starting Your Own Business: The Bestselling Guide to Planning and Building a Successful Enterprise, Jim Green, (How To Books 2005)

Resources

ARTICLE HUBS

http://ezinearticles.com

www.certificate.net/wwio

www.ideamarketers.com

www.marketing-seek.com

www.goarticles.com

www.netterweb.com

www.articlesfactory.com

http://homeincome.com/writers-connection

www.web-source.net/syndicator_submit.htm

www.searchwarp.com

www.addme.com

www.etext.org

www.zinos.com

www.vectorcentral.com

www.webpronews.com

www.writersdigest.com

www.linksnoop.com

www.articlehub.com

www.freelancewriting.com/newssyndicator.html

http://writingcorner.com/admin/sub-guidelines.htm

www.abundancecenter.com

theezine.net

www.home-based-business-opportunities.com/library/id2101-book.shtml

www.entrepreneurnewz.com

www.homebasedbusinessindex.com

www.homeincome.com

www.masterhomebusiness.com

www.articlejackpot.com

www.articlelookup.com

www.articlemill.com

www.articlenexus.com

www.articlepoint.com

www.articletime.com

www.articletogo.com

www.articlewarehouse.com

www.articlebliss.com

www.articlewarehouse.com

www.article-content-king.com

www.articlecrazy.com

www.article-direct.com

www.article-directory.com

www.articlefinders.com

www.article-highway.com

www.articlepeak.com

www.articlepros.com

www.articlesmagazine.com

www.articles411.com

www.articles4business.com

www.articlesfactory.com

www.articleshaven.com

www.articleshelf.com

www.articleshow.com

www.articles.net

www.articlesphere.com

www.articlevenue.com

www.article-warehouse.com

www.articlewiz.com

www.authorconnection.com

www.bharatbhasha.com

www.bigarticles.com

www.blogwidow.com

www.blogtelecast.com

www.businessknow-how.com

www.businessknowledgesource.com

www.businessopportunity.com

www.businesstoolchest.com

www.chiff.com

www.clearviewpublications.com

www.commonconnections.com

www.content-articles.com

www.contentdesk.com

www.contentmasterworld.com

www.cumuli.com

www.digitalwomen.com

www.directarticles.com

www.ebookdeals.com

www.ebusiness-articles.com

www.e-calc.net

www.e-syndicate.com

www.ezau.com

www.ezinecrow.com

www.ezine-writer.com.au

www.FBCmarketing.com

www.freearticlezone.com

www.freesticky.com

www.freeezinesite.com

www.fresh-articles.com

www.getyourarticles.com

www.goodinfo.com

www.homebiztools.com

www.homebusinessdigest.com

www.homebusinesswebsite.com

www.howtoadvice.com

www.homebiztools.com

www.how-it-works.net

www.ibizresources.com

www.internetbasedmoms.com

www.jogena.com

www.learningfolder.com

www.linkgrinder.com

www.marketingtroll.com

www.mbnet.com

www.more4youarticledirectory.com

www.morganadvicearchive.com

www.NADmedia.com

www.newarticlesonline.com

www.newfreearticles.com

www.onlinelists.com

www.powerhomebiz.com

www.promotiondata.com

www.purplehelp.com

www.rapidaticle.com

www.reprintarticles.com

www.simplysearch4it.com

www.smallbusinessportal.com

www.storebuilder.com

www.submit-your-articles.com

www.success4youmarketing.com

www.theezinedot.net

www.wordpress.com

www.uncoverthenet.com

www.uniterra.com

www.upromote.com

www.webmarketingspecialists.com

www.webpromotionguru.com

www.webreference.com

www.webmasterslibrary.com

www.websitetrafficinfo.com

www.websitefuel.com

www.workoninternet.com

AUTHOR'S SELF-HELP WEBSITES

http://howtoproducts-xl.com

http://howtoproducts-xl.com/2.html

http://howtoproducts-xl.com/ccc.html

http://howtoproducts-xl.com/madhatter.html

http://howtoproducts-xl.com/niche.html

http://howtobecomefamousonline.howtoproducts-xl.com

http://weboptimization.howtoproducts-xl.com

http://1st-creative-writing-course.com

http://1st-creative-writing-course.com/gettingpublished.html

http://1st-creative-writing-course.com/homeshopoffice/online.html

http://1st-creative-writing-course.com/makemoney.html

http://1st-creative-writing-course.com/mistakes/acm.html

http://1st-creative-writing-course.com/progress/pro.html

http://1st-creative-writing-course.com/starting/starting.html

http://1st-creative-writing-course.com/wfp.html

http://costcutters.howtoproducts-xl.com

http://makingmoneyonline-xl.com

http://retirement-moneymakers.com

http://start-a-business-masterplan.com

http://free-stuff-xl.com

AUTO-RESPONDERS

www.aweber.com

www.getresponse.com

www.autobots.net

www.autoresponders.com

www.freeautobot.com

www.ultimateresponse.com

CHECKING ON LINKS

www.htmltoolbox.com

CONSUMER REVIEWS

www.consumerreview.com

www.consumersearch.com

www.consumersdigest.com

DIGITAL BOOK CREATORS

www.ebookcovergenerator.com

www.ebookgenerator.com

www.adobe.com

www.deskPDF.com

DOMAIN NAMES

www.OpenForSale.com

www.whois.com

EBOOK COVER GENERATORS

www.virtualcovercreator.com

EZINE ANNOUNCEMENT LISTS

List_Builder-subscribe@topica.com

http://groups.yahoo.com

EZINE DIRECTORIES

www.bestezines.com

www.ezineaction.com

www.ezineadvertising.com

www.ezine-dir.com

www.ezinelibrary.com

www.ezinelocater.com

www.ezine-marketing.com

www.ezinesearch.com

www.ezinestoday.com

www.ezine-swap.com

www.ezine-universe.com

E-SERVICE

www.rightnowtechnologies.com

FORUMS

www.forumone.com

KEYWORD EFFECTIVENESS TOOL

http://mikes-marketing-tools.com

KEYWORD RESEARCH REPORTS

www.seoresearchlabs.com

KEYWORD SELECTION TOOLS

www.goodkeywords.com

http://inventory.overture.com/d/searchinventory/suggestion/

www.wordtracker.com

www.adwordanalyzer.com

LINK BUILDING INSTRUCTION

www.linking101.com

www.linkingmatters.com

ONLINE CREDIT CARD PROCESSORS

www.clickbank.com

www.paypal.com

ONLINE PRESS RELEASE TOOLS

http://www.prweb.com

www.free-press-release.com

ONLINE DISCUSSION GROUPS

www.deja.com

www.talkcity.com

www.insidetheweb.com

www.forumone.com

www.searchengineforums.com/bin/Ultimate.cgi

MAILING LISTS

www.liszt.com

NEWSGROUPS

http://groups.google.com

SPAM FILTERS

http://spamcheck.sitesell.com

WEB HOSTING

www.sitesell.com/interactive1.html

http://thirdspherehosting.com/plus/?xstcreat&id=xstcreat&pkg=

www.hosting.com

Virtual bookmarks

This is a selection of 'golden' virtual bookmarks you won't find anywhere else – try as you may to locate them. They come with the compliments of my good friend Ewan Chia, Founder, www.midastouchmarketing.com.

MARKET RESEARCH

Here are some places for researching hot niche markets and getting ideas for products.

ClickBank Marketplace

www.clickbank.com/marketplace.com

Amazon

www.amazon.com

Barnes and Noble

www.barnesandnoble.com

Magazines.com

www.magazines.com

eBay

www.ebay.com

eBay Hot Items Report

http://pages.ebay.com/sellercenter/hotitems.pdf

eBay Research Tools

www.terapeak.com

Yahoo! Shopping

www.shopping.yahoo.com/

Yahoo! Buzz

http://buzz.yahoo.com/buzz_log

Lycos Top 50 Daily Report

http://50.lycos.com

The Ever Essential Google

www.google.com

Midas Touch Marketing Niche Keyword Suggestion Tool

www.midastouchmarketing.com/cgi-bin/key/nichekeywords.cgi

Overture Keyword Selector Tool

http://inventory.overture.com/d/searchinventory/suggestion

Overture Keyword Bid Tool

http://uv.bidtool.overture.com/d/USm/search/tools/bidtool

Google Adword Traffic Estimator Sandbox

https://adwords.google.com/select/Login3

Digital Point Keyword Tracker

www.digitalpoint.com/tools/keywords

MARKET NEWS

Where you can go to get updates on what's happening in the marketing.

Clickz Network: Solution for Marketers

www.clickz.com

Jupiter Research Business Intelligence for Business Results

www.jupiterresearch.com

Starting Your Own Business

http://entrepreneurs.about.com

Inc.com – Resource for Growing Companies

www.inc.com/home/

DM News – Online Newspaper for Direct Marketers

www.dmnews.com

Topix Direct Marketing News

www.topix.net/business/direct-marketing

Direct Marketing Association

www.the-dma.org/

COPYWRITING

Copywriting is one of the most crucial and profitable skills a marketer can have. These websites provide some of the best resources to better your own copywriting ability …

Essential Swipe File no. 1 *

www.OHPDirect.com

Essential Swipe File no. 2 *

www.TRSDirect.com

Essential Swipe File no. 3 *

www.OTSDirect.com

* Look under the 'products' section of the sales letter for these files

Rare Swipe Files from the Legends of Advertising

www.hardtofindads.com

Marketing Notebooks of a Master Wordsmith

http://masterwordsmith.blogspot.com

The Gary Halbert Letter

www.thegaryhalbertletter.com

Copywriters Board Forum

www.copywritersboard.com

Search for copies of your own web pages to spot plagiarism

www.copyscape.com

RESOURCES

Free easy website page builder

www.easy-web-page-creator.com

Free software video tutorials

www.graburl.com/videos.htm

Free online courses

www.coursesuseek.com

Summarise the content from any website

www.copernic.com/en/products/summarizer/index.html

Direct-to-desktop content

www.charlwood.com/tristana/download

Manage your Google Adsense Adwords

www.googedit.com/freeware/g_edit.exe

Sitemap generator – online

www.xml-sitemaps.com

Free Sitemap generator – desktop

http://gsitecrawler.com/f/download-
    start.asp?p=GSiteCrawler&tw=full

Create your own dynamic tutorials for free

www.wintotal.de/server/wink15-1.zip

Free DVD creator software

www.download-software-free.com/software/sdvdc.exe

Cpanel tutorial videos

www.digitallyjustified.com/howto.php

Photoshop + website design videos and tutorials

www.designsbymark.com/freetips/index.html

Content management system

http://clevercopy.bestdirectbuy.com/downloads.php

Open source scripts

www.maguma.com/Studio_Overview.506.0.html

Handwritten fonts

www.vLetter.com

Online text formatter

www.fwointl.com/FWOFormatter.html

Free press release software

www.ducttapemarketing.com/Instant-Press-Release.htm

Free Google Adword Landing Page Creator

www.landingpagebuilder.com

Cute PDF creator

www.cutepdf.com/index.htm

Free PDF 995 creator

www.pdf995.com

Jaws PDF creator

www.jawspdf.com

Photoplus – free alternative to PhotoShop

www.freeserifsoftware.com

GMIP – free alternative to PhotoShop

www.gimp.org

Free spam checker

http://spamcheck.sitesell.com

Free privacy policy generator

www.easyriver.com/myprivacy.htm

Free disclaimer generator

http://209.204.219.152/free_disclaimer.htm

MISCELLANEOUS

URL shortening service

www.grabURL.com

Deleted domain gold mine

www.justdropped.com

Cheap domain names

www.namecheap.com

Online Google page rank check

http://rankwhere.com/google-page-rank.php

Outsourcing services

www.workaholics4hire.com

Affiliate programmes directory

www.associateprograms.com

Lifetime commissions

www.lifetimecommissions.com

Bulk domain search

www.101domain.com/domain.htm

Free marketing interview audios

www.hardtofindseminars.com/AudioclipsG.htm

The E-Code Secret Internet Marketing Forum

www.The-E-Code.com/forum

Index